The Young Adult's Guide to
SAYING NO

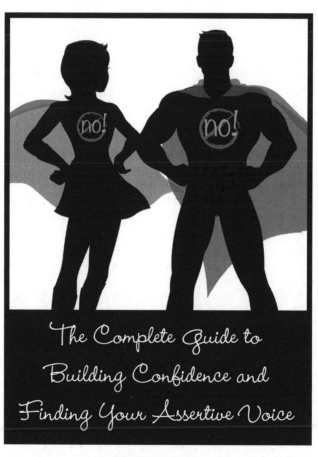

The Complete Guide to Building Confidence and Finding Your Assertive Voice

By Rebekah Sack

THE YOUNG ADULT'S GUIDE TO SAYING NO: THE COMPLETE GUIDE TO BUILDING CONFIDENCE AND FINDING YOUR ASSERTIVE VOICE

Copyright © 2016 Atlantic Publishing Group, Inc.
1405 SW 6th Avenue • Ocala, Florida 34471 • Phone 800-814-1132 • Fax 352-622-1875
Web site: www.atlantic-pub.com • E-mail: sales@atlantic-pub.com
SAN Number: 268-1250

Library of Congress Cataloging-in-Publication Data

Names: Atlantic Publishing Group, issuing body.
Title: The young adult's guide to saying no: the complete guide to building confidence and finding your assertive voice.
Description: Ocala, Florida : Atlantic Publishing Group, Inc., [2016] I
   Includes bibliographical references and index.
Identifiers: LCCN 2015035964I ISBN 9781601389893 (alk. paper) I ISBN
   1601389892 (alk. paper)
Subjects: LCSH: Assertiveness in adolescence--Juvenile literature. I
   Self-confidence in adolescence--Juvenile literature.
Classification: LCC BF724.3.A77 Y68 2016 I DDC 158.2--dc23 LC record available at http://lccn.loc.gov/2015035964

Printed in the United States

Reduce. Reuse.
RECYCLE.

A decade ago, Atlantic Publishing signed the Green Press Initiative. These guidelines promote environmentally friendly practices, such as using recycled stock and vegetable-based inks, avoiding waste, choosing energy-efficient resources, and promoting a no-pulping policy. We now use 100-percent recycled stock on all our books. The results: in one year, switching to post-consumer recycled stock saved 24 mature trees, 5,000 gallons of water, the equivalent of the total energy used for one home in a year, and the equivalent of the greenhouse gases from one car driven for a year.

Over the years, we have adopted a number of dogs from rescues and shelters. First there was Bear and after he passed, Ginger and Scout. Now, we have Kira, another rescue. They have brought immense joy and love not just into our lives, but into the lives of all who met them.

We want you to know a portion of the profits of this book will be donated in Bear, Ginger and Scout's memory to local animal shelters, parks, conservation organizations, and other individuals and nonprofit organizations in need of assistance.

*— **Douglas & Sherri Brown,***
President & Vice-President of Atlantic Publishing

Table of Contents

Chapter 2: Dealing with Negativity 35

Chapter 3: Building Your Confidence ...53

Chapter 4: Learning to Say NO 73

Chapter 5: Saying No to Friends 87

Chapter 6: Saying No to Family 103

Chapter 7: Saying No in a Relationship 111

Chapter 8: Saying No at Work and School **121**

Chapter 9: An Ongoing Plan **139**

Author's Note

know what it's like to be a people pleaser. You help other people and do thing after thing for them, and before you know it, your room is a mess, your homework isn't done, and even your hair is a little greasy.

Once, I lent money to a co-worker. She came up to me and said, "Hey, I have a huge favor to ask of you."

I braced myself, because that's a phrase I'd heard more than once in life. And by once, I mean maybe a couple of hundred times (catch that reference?).

"What is it?" I said.

"I'm in a rough spot right now and need to get groceries for me and my daughter. Could you spare a 20? I'll pay you back tomorrow; I promise."

The way she had worded her plea felt like I was already obligated to say "yes." I didn't really have any money to spare myself, but saying "no" to food for a starving child? I felt bad, like *really* bad, but I knew my way out. I fed her my excuse, which was true, I might add.

"I would, but I don't have any cash on me right now. I'm sorry."

Here I was, giving my excuse and apologizing for something that I had nothing to be sorry for. And here's the problem with giving an excuse — the other person *always* has a solution.

"There's an ATM in the lobby."

If I fed her another excuse, I would look stupid. At this point, I couldn't really say "no," because I had just said I would if I could.

So, I said the only thing I can think of. "Yeah, but the ATM charges a fee."

She didn't care. "It's only like two or three dollars."

So, there I was, walking up to the ATM and cashing out a crisp $20 bill.

I handed it to her, she said, "Thank you," and she was on her way.

Well, the next day of work comes around. We work our shift together, and I patiently waited for the "here's your money back" moment. It didn't seem like it would come.

She was gathering up her things at the front of the store, and I made sure to position myself close to her. She was putting on her jacket, getting her purse all situated, and she noticed me.

"Oh, here, let me pay you back."

I was honestly surprised. The other people I worked with told me the night before that I'd be lucky if I got my money back. Apparently she was known for asking people for money and not paying them back.

She handed me a $20, and I bit my tongue. Why didn't I ask her for the money to cover the ATM fee? I felt awkward, and I let it go.

The moral of my story is that I'm a sucker. I always give in to people, no matter the request.

In fact, one time I almost quit my job because of an unfair situation. I applied somewhere else, was hired, and went into the office to put in my two week notice.

Well, the next thing I knew, I was saying "yes" to staying and "no" to the extremely nice man that had hired me elsewhere!

It wasn't what I wanted (and things did end up working out in case you were worried), but the point is, I needed to learn how to say "no" to people.

Other people will continue to ask me for things — some will be things that I can help with, and others will be things that I will need to decline — but I wrote this book for those people out there like me (the people pleasers). We need to learn how to draw out that little guy called "confidence," and let him speak up for once.

Here is your complete guide to doing just that.

Introduction

ave you ever owned an Apple product? An iPod, an iPhone, an iPad, an iMac? Have you ever noticed the design of Apple products — very simple and minimal with no real way to customize or complicate the design?

That design was a choice made by Steve Jobs. We may not realize it, but that design choice, the reason Apple is now worth more than $700 billion, is a result of Jobs saying "no."

In a Q&A session from 1997, Jobs famously said, "You think focusing is about saying 'yes.' Focusing is about saying 'no.'" He went on to say that the people before him were working on 18 different projects, which seemed to make sense when you really looked into them, but he dared to take a step back and see what the main goal was.

He started saying "no" to those extra projects, and he put more of his time and effort into a select few.

He had to deal with people getting mad at him and the press talking trash about him and his company, but in the end, he was running one of the most successful companies in the world.

Have you ever found yourself in a situation where you were saying "yes" to someone when you really wanted to say "no"?

What about that co-worker who always asks you to pick up his Saturday night shift?

"Please? I'll owe you one!"

What about your mom who always asks you to pick up your brother from soccer practice?

"Please, honey? You can't just do this one thing for me?"

What about that teacher who keeps bugging you to join Scholastic Bowl?

"You know, we could really use you on the team."

If situations like these have happened or keep happening to you, you need to learn the power of saying "no."

You should always be your first priority. If you've ever been on a plane, you may remember the pre-flight safety demonstration where the flight attendants stand up and show you how to use your seat belt, the exits, and so on.

When they get to the oxygen masks, they tell you to set yours up first so that you can get the oxygen you need before you help anyone else. This is in the event of a life or death situation, and the standard is still to help yourself before helping anyone else.

This isn't a new idea — psychologists across the world will tell you that you have to help yourself before helping other people (even Oprah says it, so it must be true, right?).

In other words, when you actually want to say "no," you need to learn how to do it. This book is going to teach you how to say "no" to people. To do that, you have to build self-confidence and self-esteem, which will help you find your assertive voice. Throughout the course of this book, we're going to teach you how to do both of these things.

You will learn how much self-confidence and self-esteem you have as well as how to get more (it's not as hard as it sounds). Negativity can have a huge impact on your confidence, which might be why you find it hard to stand up for yourself. We'll take a look at the different kinds of negativity that might be in your life and how to get rid of it, once and for all.

Once the negativity is gone, you will learn how to build up your self-confidence. There are lots of strategies out there that give you the confidence to stand up to anyone, including people that are really close to you.

There are sample situations sprinkled throughout the book that you can look through to get an idea of how to handle some situations that you might be dealing with.

You will feel better and more confident knowing that the people who really care about you will understand that sometimes you just have to say "no." Those around you will understand that it's nothing personal if you use the tips and tricks within this book. When you start saying "no" with confidence, you'll wish you'd done it much sooner. (Oh, what a relief it is — you sang that, didn't you?)

What is Self-Confidence?

In order to feel comfortable saying "no" to people in your life, you need to build up your self-confidence. So, what exactly is self-confidence?

The logical place to start is to see how dictionaries define the word.

The Miriam-Webster dictionary defines self-confidence as "confidence in oneself and in one's powers and abilities."

Don't you hate it when dictionaries use the word they're supposed to be defining in the definition itself?

What about Dictionary.com? "Realistic confidence in one's own judgment, ability, power, etc."

There seems to be a trend here.

Let's look at the trusty Oxford English Dictionary. "Confidence in oneself; often in an unfavorable sense; arrogant or impudent reliance on one's own powers."

Woah — seems like the definition needs a little bit of defining, doesn't it? You also might notice that this definition seems to describe self-confidence as a negative thing (like it's something we don't want).

If we take all of these definitions and smack them together, what do we get? It's safe to say that self-confidence is the ability to trust or rely on yourself and your abilities (which can sometimes go overboard and turn into arrogance).

That's not such a bad thing, is it? If you can't trust in yourself and everything that you're capable of, how on earth do you expect yourself to say "no" to the people in your life? You need to have faith in yourself, and don't worry, we'll teach you how to do that.

What is Self-Esteem?

What's the difference between self-confidence and self-esteem? You know the drill; let's see what the dictionaries have to say.

Miriam-Webster says, "A feeling of having respect for yourself and your abilities."

Dictionary.com says, "A realistic respect for or favorable impression of oneself; self-respect."

The OED says, "Favorable appreciation or opinion of oneself."

Smack them all together and what do you get? Self-esteem is liking and respecting yourself. This is not a bad thing — in fact, if you don't have self-esteem, you're at risk for all kinds of negative effects in your life, which we'll get to in Chapter 2.

If you put self-confidence and self-esteem side by side, you see that having both means that you trust, rely on, like, and respect yourself and what you are capable of.

According to Glenn R. Schiraldi, Ph.D. (2007), there are two ways to measure self-esteem: he refers to them as "the core self" and "externals." To make this easier to understand, we're going to call them your inner self and your outer self. Your inner self refers to your ability to do things that make you human, like loving, thinking, and sacrificing. You will always be capable of doing these things, which gives you worth that won't go away, no matter what you do.

I know this sounds a little confusing, but all of this basically means that you, as a person, aren't capable of being worthless, because you will always have these qualities inside of you.

The world we live in likes to focus on the outer self, which refers to things like looks and social status. These things affect the way we experience our worth (if you're poor, it changes the way you think, for example), but it doesn't affect our actual worth.

If those outside things are bad, it can affect how we feel about our inner worth, causing us to have low self-esteem.

Still with me?

Here's an example if you're totally lost.

Meet Rachel. Rachel has been physically abused by her alcoholic father since she was a toddler. Because of the abuse by her father, she now believes that she is a horrible person — the abuse has led her to believe that inside, she is worthless or defective in some way.

Anyone can see that this isn't the case — Rachel is still able to do all of those things that give her worth (love, think, and sacrifice, for example), but because of the things happening outside of her core, she is led to believe otherwise. Rachel has low self-esteem because of this.

You can substitute any name and any situation — Mike is over-weight, Laura grew up in a poor neighborhood, Jonathan was sexually abused as a child — any outside force can make any person feel the way that Rachel feels.

In order to stand up for yourself, you have to have self-esteem, no matter what you've been through or what your circumstances are. You won't feel comfortable telling that co-worker "no" if you don't trust and believe in yourself.

It's important to note that having self-esteem doesn't mean that you're selfish or arrogant. Loving yourself doesn't mean that you're full of yourself. In fact, it's a lot easier to be selfless and humble when you feel secure in who you are.

In order to build yourself up, you need to know what you're working with. Read on to evaluate how confident you are and what level of self-esteem you have.

Chapter 1

Who You Are

In order to move forward and correct the problem, you need to know what the problem is. Maybe you don't have an issue with confidence or self-esteem, but odds are, you do even if you think you don't. Statistics are hard to come by when it comes to self-esteem — sources tend say that somewhere around 85 percent of the population has low self-esteem.

It's hard to calculate how many of us have self-esteem issues, because it's hard to measure. How low is too low? Who decides? My psychiatrist or me? How many people in the world actually see a psychiatrist?

The point is, we can all safely agree that the majority of the population deals with self-esteem issues. That means that while most of us have a problem, there are some people that simply don't.

Am I Naturally Confident?

From Justin Bieber to Demi Lovato, it seems like just about everyone is talking (well, singing) about being confident. If you are naturally confident, you're a pretty rare specimen.

If you're confident, you:

- Appreciate your talents
- Are a generally positive person
- Say "thank you" when someone compliments you
- Aren't afraid to talk about your strengths
- Welcome feedback
- Generally don't care about what people think of you
- Don't constantly fear rejection

How many of these describe you?

Take the third point, for example — you say "thank you" when someone compliments you. Your crush at school notices your new haircut. He or she says, "Wow. Nice haircut. Looks great," or, "Oh my gosh, that new haircut looks really nice — where did you go?"

What do you do? Do you try to diffuse the compliment by saying something like, "Oh, this haircut? It's not exactly how I wanted it, but hair grows back out."

Do you feel most comfortable throwing the compliment back by saying something like, "My haircut? Look at yours!"

If you're confident, you probably answer with a calm and composed "thank you."

You can also go a step too far by being arrogant with a response like, "I know."

If you tend to diffuse a compliment, you need to work on your self-confidence. Finding the line between high self-confidence and arrogance is the key to being successful, especially when it comes to finding your assertive voice.

Let's take a look at another example — you don't constantly fear rejection.

The school talent show is coming up. You're an amazing musician, but you are trying to decide if you should even be in the talent show. What do you do when someone asks you?

a) You say, "Eh, I don't know. I get really nervous in front of other people."

b) You say, "Me? Join the talent show? What about you? You're a great dancer. You should really do it this year."

c) You say, "You know what? I think I will."

d) You say, "Did you really think I wouldn't? Someone has to win these things."

You can probably guess where this is going. If you're most likely to do **a**, you tend to fear rejection. Answer **b** is another way of diffusing the limelight off of yourself, which is a sign that you need to work on your confidence. If you chose **c**, you're on the right track. If you chose **d**, well, I think we all see the problem with person **d**.

Take a close look at each bullet point again. How do you usually respond to these things? Are you uncomfortable talking about your 4.0 GPA? Do you leave that new shirt at home because you're afraid people at school will make fun of it? Do you find yourself getting into these dark, slumpy moods (yes, I just made up the word slumpy) that feel impossible to get out of?

If these kinds of things tend to describe you, you definitely have low self-confidence and need to take the confidence-building suggestions in Chapter 3 pretty seriously (particularly the hard tasks).

If one or two of the bullet points describe you, then you are in a good place, but you still have room to improve (don't we all?).

Do I Have Low Self-Esteem?

It's important to know that if you do have low-esteem, you're normal. The Center for Mental Health Services (2003) explains, "Some self-doubt, particularly during adolescence, is normal — even healthy — but poor self-esteem should not be ignored."

Even the experts say that it's totally normal for you to be struggling with this. The thing is, living with low self-esteem stinks, which is why you need to find out if you have it so that you can reverse it and begin to love yourself.

The Self-Esteem Institute TM, founded by Dr. Sorenson, explains that if you have low self-esteem, you're often struggling with the following:

- Panic attacks

- Extreme anxiety

- Fear, in general

- Depression

- Hypersensitivity (super sensitive and easily offended)

- Hypervigilence (feeling inadequate, like you don't fit in)

- Lack of assertiveness (being passive, giving in to others easily)

- Lack of self-confidence

- OCD

- Addiction

- Workaholic behavior

- Either an underachiever or an overachiever (one of the two extremes)

- Poor boundaries (can't make choices, feel like you can't share your feelings)

- Bad social skills (find it hard to make friends)

- Self-sabotaging (acting in ways that clearly aren't in your own best interest)

- Sexual dysfunction

- Unreasonable expectations (expecting other people to know what you're thinking)

This list is pretty heavy duty — there are some real issues in there that can be both hard to live with and hard to admit. It's clear that self-esteem is a bigger and deeper issue than self-confidence, though both are closely related in nature.

There are some specific symptoms of low self-esteem in there that directly explain why you might find it difficult to stand up for what you want. Take fear, for example. Let's turn to a case study from a new middle school teacher to see how fear can affect us.

CASE STUDY: CLAIRE, FIRST-YEAR MIDDLE SCHOOL TEACHER

At the end of the school year breakfast, the principal announced to everyone that I would be the music, Spanish, *and* drama teacher. Well, this was news to me.

As soon as he announced that I was going to teach drama, the lady in charge of running Vacation Bible School came across the auditorium and asked me if I could run the drama room. She said that the lady who usually did it couldn't this year. She told me the dates, and it conflicted with the date of my mom having surgery.

They told me that I would have a parent working the room with me, so she could be in charge while I was at the hospital with my mom. I was really uncomfortable. I hadn't had any previous drama experience, but I felt that I had to say "yes," because I was the new teacher and a new member of the community. I felt that if I said "no," I would be making a bad impression, and I would lose respect from parents, peers, and co-workers in the year to follow.

So, despite every ounce of my body wanting to say "no," I said "yes." And I regretted it. As a trained musician, putting something on stage that isn't good or ready (to your standard, which is usually a higher standard than the average person) kills you on the inside. Along with that, the kids were crazy and misbehaved, my drama team was just as clueless as I was, my parent volunteer thought everything was a joke, and to top it off, my mom was having surgery.

My mom has always told me, and still tells me that "no" is a complete sentence, and that I don't need to explain myself. Sometimes that's a lot easier said than done, especially with peer pressure and constant nagging.

If I could go back, I definitely would have said "no." However, I feel like I would have really had to give a good reason or explanation. I would have had to use my mom having surgery as a huge selling point. I feel like if I just said "no" without an excuse, that wouldn't have been received well.

Claire had a fear of being rejected and of losing respect. When you're new at a place, it feels like you need to do a lot of extra things to be respected and taken seriously. However, what happened in the end was worse than Claire's initial fear.

Another example from the list that explains why you're finding it hard to stand up to other people's requests is lack of assertiveness. Being assertive means being bold. If you aren't assertive, the spiral goes downhill pretty quickly.

fears upsetting others
> becomes passive
> anger builds up
> explosion happens

The explosion could be anything that's a result of built-up anger. You could become sarcastic, aggressive, rude, brusque (being short or abrupt with people), or even violent.

You got that right — continuing to say "yes" to people when you really want to say "no" can turn you into a scary version of yourself.

It's possible that you can also develop passive-aggressive behavior when you don't find your assertive voice. If you've never heard that term before, you're probably familiar with it and just don't realize it. Here's an example that anyone who had ever had a fight with a S.O. will probably recognize.

A boy and a girl are in an argument.

Boy: "I'm just saying that that's how I feel."
Girl: *Clearly upset.* "Whatever."

It's as simple as that. The girl withdraws herself from the argument and pretends like she isn't angry, when in reality, the boy knows that she is.

Here's another example.

Mom: Can you clean your room please?
Son: *Puts on a huge smile and uses a very chipper voice.* "Sure, I'd be happy to!"

This is sometimes called "the angry smile." The son is pretending like he's very cooperative and happy to do what his mother asked, when in reality, he's angry and doesn't want to do it at all.

Now, we aren't saying you should find your assertive voice and tell your mom to back off when she asks you to clean your room (definitely don't do that!). That was just an example of passive-aggressive behavior.

All jokes aside, this kind of behavior makes you a really unlikable person.

Back to the bullet points. The symptoms of low self-esteem are pretty serious in comparison with low self-confidence. If you have even one of these symptoms, you need to pay attention to the hard tasks in Chapter 3, specifically seeing a counselor or therapist.

Issues like OCD, panic attacks, and depression can take over your life pretty quickly. Prescription drugs are never the only answer, but they do exist for conditions like these, which should tell you that you need to take them very seriously. It's possible that you won't be able to kick some of these symptoms off by yourself. Don't be afraid to ask other people to help you. You don't want to turn into a passive-aggressive or even violent person because of low self-esteem.

Moving Forward

Go back through the bullet points and circle the ones that speak to you. If you find it difficult to acknowledge your strengths, circle that point. If you think you're hypersensitive, circle it. Hold the book back and see how many circles you have and think about how big those issues are.

Most of the low self-confidence issues can be worked on with the easy tasks in Chapter 3. However, remember that even one of the low self-*esteem* issues will need to be taken very seriously with one or all of the hard tasks in Chapter 3.

Even if your problems seem small, sometimes we do need that unbiased, outside opinion to give us the hard truth. Consider talking with a counselor even if you think you're fine.

The first step is simply finding your weaknesses. If you can point out what you're struggling with, you're one step closer to fixing it.

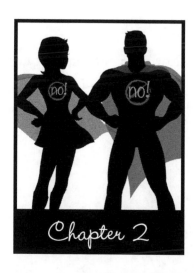

Chapter 2

Dealing with Negativity

I f reading about negativity is weighing you down, you can imagine what living with it every day feels like. In this chapter, we're going to discover what negativity is (maybe you're dealing with it and don't realize it) and the effects it can have on your life (it isn't pretty).

We're going to take a look at negative self-talk and social anxiety. Skip to the end to see how this kind of negativity can affect you at your present and in your future.

Negative Self-Talk

Roger Ebert (1942-2013) was arguably one of the most famous movie critics of all time. He was known for getting down to the tough truth — and he certainly wasn't shy about it.

TIME Magazine's Nolan Feeney outlines some of his most brutal reviews of all time:

> 1) "Valentine's Day": "'Valentine's Day' is being marketed as a Date Movie. I think it's more of a First-Date Movie. If your date likes it, do not date that person again. And if you like it, there may not be a second date."

2) "North": "I hated this movie. Hated hated hated hated hated this movie. Hated it. Hated every simpering stupid vacant audience-insulting moment of it. Hated the sensibility that thought anyone would like it. Hated the implied insult to the audience by its belief that anyone would be entertained by it."

3) "Transformers: Revenge of the Fallen": "[The movie] is a horrible experience of unbearable length, briefly punctuated by three or four amusing moments. One of these involves a dog-like robot humping the leg of the heroine. Such are the meager joys."

4) "Police Academy": "It's so bad, maybe you should pool your money and draw straws and send one of the guys off to rent it so that in the future, whenever you think you're sitting through a bad comedy, he could shake his head, and chuckle tolerantly, and explain that you don't know what bad is."

Woah, some of those are pretty vicious. I wonder how it would feel to be on the receiving end of those insults? I think you see where this is going.

When you deal with negative self-talk, it's like you have your own personal Roger Ebert in your ear, whispering cruel criticism to you all day long. Now, not to say that Ebert never had great movie reviews, because he did (he wasn't *always* negative).

However, when you constantly put yourself down, that's kind of what it's like.

There's nothing wrong with some self-criticism every once in a while. Sometimes we need to kick ourselves in the behind to get motivated. However, there's a big difference between saying, "I need to get my hair cut" and "I look like I just got electrocuted."

To be better people, we need to touch on our failures and work on improving them. The difference between healthy and disastrous is when you dwell on the failures for far too long.

So, how do we change the way we think from "I'm a fat blob" to "I should work out more?"

Here are some tips to channel your inner positive thinker.

Stopping negative self-talk

There are a lot of things you can do to become an all-around more positive person. They do require a little bit of work, but know that you have the power to stop the negative self-talk as long as you put in a conscious effort.

1) Set goals

It's easy to say "I'll just start thinking more positively," but realistically, this probably won't do much for you.

Accomplishing things makes us feel more positive, so by setting goals and actually reaching them, we start to become more positive people. Brian Masters, author of *Positive Thinking* (2016), explains that if you set short-term goals, you'll start to kick that habit of negative self-talk.

He says, "In order to choose a short term goal, think about a situation that happened recently that caused you to engage in negative self-talk. It is best if you think of an everyday sort of situation that happens frequently in your life, or at least is likely to happen again in the near future."

So, what's getting you down? If it's your weight, set a short-term goal. For example, a short-term goal could be going for a walk in the morning or avoiding soda for the day. By setting the goal and then actually achieving it, you're throwing that negative self-talk in the dumpster (and slamming the lid).

Once you start to master these short-term goals, step it up to longer ones. You've mastered the morning walk and the ridding of soda — you're ready for the next step. To set a long-term goal, you might set up a nutrition plan or go to the gym and get a membership.

By taking physical action toward completing these goals, you are engaging in more positive thinking, which will eventually give you the power to kick out that negative self-talk for good.

If organization or to-do lists motivate you, create one. Check off the completed goals to feel an immediate sense of satisfaction and positivity.

2) Pinpoint your mental trigger

What exactly is that negative thought that causes the downward spiral of negative self-talk? If you pinpoint it, you can move forward with clearing it up.

Let's continue with the weight example. Let's name our example figure "Mara." Mara struggles with her weight. When she thinks about working out, she starts out with the thought, "I hate exercising because it hurts and is uncomfortable. I'd rather stay at home and catch up on my favorite TV show."

That line of thinking is Mara's mental trigger.

```
                    Exercise hurts
           > I'll never be able to lose weight
               > I will hate my body forever
```

Once she can pinpoint that that's causing her downward spiral, she can decode it and figure out how to reverse it.

Masters explains what to do when you encounter a mental trigger: "Pay attention to when you experience this thought, feeling or fear and as soon as you do, remind yourself of the reasons why these fears should be ignored so you can engage in positive actions that help you achieve your goals, rather than negative actions that only further hinder your ability to think positively."

So, Mara has pinpointed her negative self-talk trigger. She's at home, she's looking at her workout gear, and she's thinking about the morning ahead.

"I know I should work out, but it's really hot outside, and running is so uncomfortable. I absolutely hate it."

Wait, Mara thinks, *this is my mental trigger.*

Mara steps back and reminds herself of the reasons why this fear should be ignored.

She knows that she wants to lose weight, and she knows that if she works out, her goal will be achieved faster than just following her diet plan. She remembers how great she feels once she's done, the endorphins flowing through her body and the sense of accomplishment running through her bones. She remembers how horrible she feels when she listens to that mental trigger and decides to stay at home and lie on the couch.

She ignores her mental trigger and puts the workout gear on. She steps out the door and lets the positive thoughts push her one more step toward her goal.

3) Consider your mental health

If you've tried these strategies before and they just aren't doing it for you, it's possible that something in your brain is still bringing you down.

If you think this might be the case, it's possible that you have a mental health issue that needs to be addressed. When we talk about mental health issues in this situation, we mean conditions like depression, anxiety, and even certain phobias.

If you aren't sure what these kinds of conditions are, we'll take a look at them in this section. If you do think that one of these describes you, you'll need to commit to seeing a counselor for help.

Social Anxiety

Social anxiety, when you break it down to its simplest definition, is when you feel like other people are constantly judging you. It's obviously more complicated than that, but that's the gist of it.

This condition can be broken down into three parts: anxious sensations, anxious thoughts, and anxious behaviors. Let's outline the main components of each part, courtesy of Social Anxiety Support (SAS).

Anxious sensations are things that happen to your body. They're the physical symptoms of social anxiety. If you have social anxiety, you'll notice the following:

- Blushing
- Sweating
- Racing heart
- Shaking or tremors
- Dry mouth
- Shortness of breath
- Feeling faint

Anxious thoughts are phrases you might be thinking in your head about yourself, other people, or the situation that you're in. They might be thoughts like:

- "Everyone is staring at me."
- "They'll think I'm a loser."
- "I don't belong here."
- "I won't have anything to say."
- "People will see how nervous I am."

- "They won't want to talk to me again."
- "I will keep looking more and more foolish."

Anxious behaviors are actions you take because of your social anxiety. They can have a huge impact on your quality of life. These behaviors include the following:

- Avoiding entering social situations
- Leaving situations
- Only entering "safe" places
- Using cellphones, headphones, or other devices to avoid being in conversations
- Apologizing all the time
- Asking for encouragement from other people
- Preparing excessively (memorizing what to say, extreme grooming)
- Trying to direct people's attention away from your performance
- Watching for signs that people are judging you

If you notice yourself dealing with a combination of things from all three of these categories, you might be dealing with social anxiety. You notice the anxiety most when you're interacting with other people or when you're forced to be the center of attention.

It's important to know that social anxiety isn't always a bad thing — it's part of being a human being. A recent survey showed that about 12 percent of people experience social anxiety (qtd. in Social Anxiety Support). However, if it's having an effect on your quality of life or holding you back from doing certain things, you need to address the fact that you have a problem (and fix it!).

If you suspect you have a problem, your first step is to see a professional. They can determine if it's a real problem, and then they'll help you treat it. The most effective treatments are medication, cognitive-behavioral therapy, or a combination of the two.

What is cognitive-behavioral therapy?

That super long term just means that you're engaging in some kind of therapy to stop unhealthy thinking and behavior. SAS explains that cognitive-behavioral therapy (CBT) is done through team-work (you and your counselor). No one just tells you what to do.

The therapy is designed to help you develop new skills that you can use to overcome your anxiety. The goal of this therapy is to help you learn what you need to be your own counselor in the future.

The therapy is very structured. Each time you see your counsel-or, you have a specific set of goals for that particular day. You usually go home with some kind of "homework," which is like an exercise that you can do in real life.

The main goal of CBT is learning how to become your own thera-pist so that you can treat yourself when you need to. There are tools out there that can help you if you want to learn how, but it's highly recommended that you see a counselor or therapist first.

SAS recommends *The Shyness and Social Anxiety Workbook: Prov-en Step-by-Step Techniques for Overcoming Your Fear* by Martin M. Antony, Ph.D., and Richard Swinson, M.D., because it has prov-en to be an effective treatment for people with social anxiety.

So, what does all of this have to do with my ability to say "no" to people? Well, if you have social anxiety, chances are your self-esteem is lower than normal. You'll find it difficult to stand up for yourself, let alone be comfortable receiving the request. If you seek out treatment that can really help you, you'll be well on your way to finding that assertive voice of yours.

Effects of Negative Self-Esteem

In case you don't think your low self-esteem is that big of a problem, keep reading to find out what it can do to you (and it's not pretty).

Unemployment

According to a study published in the Journal of Applied Economics (2015), if you have low self-esteem, you are more likely to be unemployed when you are older. This is more a problem for women than men, but it's still a problem.

It hurts you when you're interviewing, because confidence is one of the biggest things that job interviewers look for in the hiring process. They want to know that you're sure of yourself so that they can be sure of you.

It also causes people to lose their jobs once they actually have one. Low self-esteem can make it hard to respond to criticism, it can stop you from asking for what you want (can I get a raise?), and it causes you to be too hard on yourself (you're your own toughest critic).

Health problems

If you have low self-esteem, you're more likely to have physical health problems when you get older, according to a study published in Developmental Psychology (2006).

All kinds of bad things can start to happen, including poor cardiorespiratory health — that means your heart and lungs — and obesity (gaining lots of weight). These effects could lower your self-esteem even more, trapping you in a downward spiral of feeling bad. I think we can all agree that we don't want that to happen, right?

Low self-esteem can also cause poor self-perceived health when you're older, which means that you may think of yourself as fat or unhealthy (even if you aren't).

Eating problems

Having low self-esteem can cause you to have eating problems, even to the point of developing an eating disorder. One study in the International Journal of Eating Disorders (1997) asked more than 600 young girls about their self-esteem and eating habits. They found that about half of them had low self-esteem.

Over half of the girls said they felt too fat and tried to control their weight. They tried doing this in many different ways, including crazy amounts of exercise, forcing themselves to vomit, taking laxatives and water tablets, and dieting.

Nearly one in every 10 girls said they had tried induced vomiting (making yourself throw up to lose weight). The study said that this meant 7–8 percent of the girls showed evidence of a partial syndrome eating disorder.

An eating disorder is a serious illness that causes huge problems with your eating behaviors. Three of the most common eating disorders are anorexia, bulimia, and binge eating.

Anorexia

Anorexia could cause you to see yourself as fat, even if you are dangerously skinny. If you have anorexia, you might weigh yourself constantly, severely limit the amount of food you eat, and eat very small portions of food when you do eat.

Bulimia

Bulimia is when you repeatedly eat lots of food and try to make up for it by making yourself throw up. People who suffer from bulimia may also use laxatives or diuretics (those make food travel through the body faster), and they tend to work out way too much.

Binge eating

Binge eating is like bulimia without the induced vomiting or accelerated digestion. Someone who binge eats loses control over his or her eating habits, which makes him or her gain a lot of weight, causing even more self-esteem issues.

If you think you might have any of these eating disorders, you should talk to a doctor or trusted adult immediately.

Depression

If you've ever felt really sad (and I mean *really* sad) or worthless, it might be a sign that you have depression. Depression is a common but serious problem that affects millions of people around the world. According to a study published in the Journal of Abnormal Psychology (2009), low self-esteem is often related to depressive systems, no matter what your age is.

Experts say to watch out for these symptoms to find out if you might be suffering from depression:

- Constantly feeling sad
- Feeling anxious and hopeless
- Losing interest in hobbies and recreational activities
- Having difficulty sleeping

- Struggling to concentrate or focus on tasks
- Thinking often about death or suicide

The important thing to know is that your low self-esteem might not be your fault — it might be your body going a little whacko. If you think you might have some of these issues, talk to a doctor or trusted adult right away. They care about you, and they want to help.

Addiction

If you have low self-esteem, you're far more likely to abuse alcohol or drugs, according to AlcoholRehab.com. This means that you're more likely to have an addiction in the future. Let's look at another example.

Natalie has low self-esteem and isn't that confident in her ability to meet people and make friends. Someone from her class invites her to a party, and she hears there will be alcohol there. Natalie has heard that drinking can loosen you up and make you more comfortable around other people. Maybe she'll go and try it to see if it helps her make friends.

There are a lot of negative effects that drinking can have on you and your body. You've heard it before: drinking can make you sick and can lead to some pretty stupid decisions. If you're using drugs or alcohol specifically to turn yourself into "a different person," you could be at a higher risk of developing an addiction.

It can be tempting to try using drugs or alcohol to make yourself more comfortable and relaxed in social situations, but that means that you might start to rely on it. If you start drinking, you might not be able to give it up, because you'll become both physically and mentally addicted to it. Then, you'll have bigger problems than just low self-esteem.

Anti-social behavior

Imagine you are in quicksand. The more you move and struggle to escape, the faster you sink into the pit. Low self-esteem can have a similar effect on your social life. At first, you may find that you are uncomfortable being yourself around others. But, as a study in Psychological Science (2005) indicates, it can wind up causing you to externalize — or inflict on others — the self-esteem issues you are having, and it can lead to aggressive and anti-social behavior.

Here's an example. Let's name our example guy "Chris." Chris is usually uncomfortable in social situations. After a while, he's convinced that no one likes him even though he's not really trying to make friends. So, he decides he's going to just reject any friendly advances. Now, his self-esteem problem has completely changed the way he interacts with others.

As Dr. Sorenson's Self-Esteem Institute explains, this anti-social behavior can take many different forms.

For example, if you have low self-esteem, you might have a hard time deciding who you can trust and who you can't. Often, this could mean that anyone who shows kindness or attention toward you can win you over, opening you up to potential manipulation or pain. Trust is something that takes time to develop, and low self-esteem can throw off your scale.

It could also cause you to view yourself as undeserving of friendship. If you view yourself negatively, you might assume that others do, too.

Imagine that Lindsey has low self-esteem and doesn't make a lot of friends at school. One day, she drops her lunch tray in the lunchroom and many people laugh at her. This confirms (to her) that everything negative she thought about herself was true and makes her feel even worse than she already did, driving her further inward socially. Even when Lindsey is invited to a birthday party, she is entirely convinced everyone is playing a big joke on her and that no one is interested in what she has to say.

Sometimes, this intense focus on the negative aspects of every situation can lead to others viewing you as arrogant. If you have really high standards, nothing will ever satisfy you, and others may notice. If you're also worrying about negative outcomes, it can leave you frozen in fear of doing something wrong.

Here's another example. Let's name this guy "Reed." Reed is trying to decide where to go to college. His father went to State and has raised Reed as a State fan. Deep down, Reed is interested in making movies, and Tech has a great filmmaking program. After being accepted into both schools, Reed decides to go to State, because he's terrified of letting down his parents and of losing their support. In the process, he could potentially be giving up on his dream.

If you don't like and respect yourself, you won't be able to like and respect others.

Chapter 3

Building Your Confidence

uilding confidence can be really simple or really complicated — there are things you can do that are quick and simple fixes and other things that will take time and effort. If you found that you have extremely low self-esteem, then you need to focus more on the harder tasks (ugh, we know).

If you found that you struggle with self-esteem on a smaller scale, then boost what you have and sprinkle in some of the easier tasks. No matter where you stand on the self-esteem scale, taking the time to do some of these suggestions will make it easier to say "no" to someone.

Easy Tasks

These suggestions are things that are super easy — they don't require a whole lot of time and effort from you. There's no reason you shouldn't take advantage of the confidence benefits.

Wear perfume or cologne

I know what you're thinking — you really think that wearing a scent is going to make it easier for me to tell people "no"?

The short answer is yes.

In case you were wondering, the long answer comes from a study done about fragrance. Rachel S. Herz, a recognized expert on the psychology of smell, reports that both men and women feel more confident when they smell good.

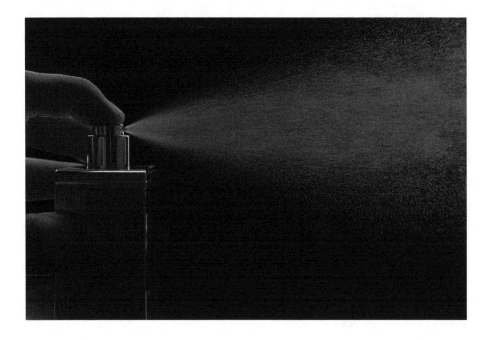

In *Neurobiology of Sensation and Reward* (2011), Herz explains a study done on men wearing scented and unscented deodorant. The men were asked how they felt after a day of wearing the scent. Herz reports, "men wearing the scented deodorant felt more confident than the unscented men." The study also found that if the guy really liked the smell, he felt even *more* confident.

Guys — choose a scented deodorant that you really like. You wear deodorant anyway (we hope), so why not boost your confidence as you do it?

The study was also done on women, and there was a similar result: "90 percent of all women tested in the fragrance study reported feeling more confident when they wore fragrance than when they did not."

Girls — spritz on a body spray or perfume. It will boost your confidence, which actually makes others find you more attractive, among other things.

The point here is that something that takes very little effort boosts your confidence, which goes beyond just smelling good. It changes the way you walk, the way you think, and most importantly how you feel about yourself. If you feel confident, it will be a lot easier to stand up for yourself.

Get to spritzing!

Sit up straight

This isn't too good to be true — having good posture increases your confidence. We turn to another study to explain it.

The American Psychological Association published a study called "Do Slumped and Upright Postures Affect Stress Responses?" (2015). In this study, researchers were trying to find out how postures affect us, specifically with stress.

When they were done, they found out that having slumped posture is a signal of depression, and upright posture is a signal of confidence.

The report says, "sitting in an erect posture did not affect participants' mood or valence of thoughts compared to a slumped posture, although it did create more confidence in thoughts."

In other words, if you sit up straight, you're more likely to think confidently.

Good posture means that you stick out your chest (comfortably) and look straight ahead. Your head should be level. Your back should be straight. Naturally we slouch a little bit, so even though it might feel like your back is curving, chances are it's finally straight.

Nod your head

If you thought spraying perfume on yourself and sitting up straight were easy, how about nodding your head?

Researchers from the Journal of Personality and Social Psychology report (2003), "results of the hierarchical regression analysis revealed a significant main effect of head movements, such that nodders showed higher confidence in their thoughts than shakers.

Also, a significant effect of reported elaboration emerged, showing that as elaboration increased, thought confidence increased."

In case you don't speak science, this means that studies show that nodding your head in a conversation boosts your confidence.

Let's apply this to the main goal of this book. For example, your classmate is explaining their sob story to you: "I was sick all weekend, and my mom was out of town, and I'm already really behind in this class, and I promise I'll never ask a favor from you again," and at this point, you've nodded your head a couple of times, and they finally blurt out their request, "can I please copy your math homework? I promise it will only take me like two minutes, and no one will see."

You're wearing a fragrance, you're sitting up straight, and you've been nodding your head in understanding, which has boosted your confidence through the roof. Saying "no" is already three times easier now than it was before.

Turn up the bass

A recent study published in Social Psychological and Personality Science (2015) found that listening to music makes you feel more confident.

They found a lot of interesting things in the study, one of which was that if you listen to music with heavier bass, it makes you feel more powerful.

The study recognizes that there are other things that make you feel more powerful, like posture, which we covered, but the most interesting and new thing that this study found is that the most "effective and convenient way" to feel powerful quickly is to listen to "high-power music," which most of the time means music with heavy bass.

If you prefer music with lighter bass, you don't have to force yourself to listen to music you don't like. There are plenty of other easy things you can do to boost your confidence, but this one was too easy to pass up.

Keep your good luck charm

Do you have a trusty necklace, a lucky hair tie, or a dependable watch? Don't toss it out just yet — studies show that having your good luck charm actually helps you do better when you're completing a task.

A study done by some professors in Germany (2010) found that when people had their good luck charm with them, they experienced an "increase in perceived level of self-efficacy."

Self-efficacy is really similar to self-esteem. Self-efficacy is when you believe that you can succeed at something.

So, in simpler words, the study found that when people had their good luck charm with them, they were more likely to feel like they could succeed. Not only did they feel like they would do better, but they actually did do better. The boost in confidence made a huge difference.

Break a sweat

It seems like exercise is the cure for just about everything, including low self-esteem. This one may seem like it's not that easy, but a recent study suggests that it's not about how hard you exercise, it's about breaking a sweat, period.

In other words, it doesn't matter if you do sprints for half or hour or do a casual morning stroll — you still benefit from the boost in confidence. The lead researcher in the study,

Russell Clayton, explains the results (2014): "Individuals who exercised regularly were more confident they could handle the interaction of their work and home life and were less likely to be stressed at work."

How exactly does this relate to you? Well, substitute what you do full time — go to school — for the full-time job, and what do you have?

Evidence suggests that if you exercise, you'll be more confident that you can handle conversations at school as well as at home, and you're less likely to be stressed at school. It's the same concept, and it still applies to you.

Exercise has been proven to reduce stress, and if you're struggling to say "no" to someone, it's possible that that's causing you stress on a daily basis.

So, if you do decide to break a sweat, not only will you be reducing stress, but you'll be building your confidence, which will make it easier for you to find your assertive voice.

Plus, you might be able to kick that stubborn tummy flab in the process.

Paint a picture of success

Visualizing an image of success actually does something, according to a recent study done by Patrick J Carroll (2014).

Here's the low down on the study. Students were asked to meet with an adviser about a fake program called "Business Psychology." The point of the test was to see how these students would react to different levels of validation from the adviser.

The students were asked to fill out some paperwork before meeting with the adviser. The paperwork asked for things like their GPA and their self-confidence.

There were four different groups. The first group of students was the control group. When they met with the adviser, nothing was said about a GPA requirement for the Business Psychology program.

The rest of the groups were told that the GPA requirement to get into the program was .10 less than what their own GPA was. In other words, they were able to apply to the program.

The second group was simply told that their GPA was over the requirement.

The third group was told that their GPA was over the requirement and that they were a shoo-in.

The fourth group was told that their GPA was over the requirement, that they were a shoo-in, that they were probably going to get full funding, that they would do amazing in the program, and that by the time they graduated, they would have tons of job offers on the table.

What Carroll found was pretty cool — only the fourth group was really interested in the program and was willing to apply to it; they also felt more self-confident about the idea. The rest of the groups said they were unlikely to apply to the program.

So, what does this study mean for you?

If you visualize a really specific, clear image in your head of where you want to end up or how you want things to go, chances are, you'll be more confident about it.

Long story short? Visualize saying "no," and you'll feel more confident when the time comes to actually do it.

Smile

We saved the easiest for last. The simple task of smiling does amazing things for you and your brain — studies show that smiling can reduce stress, it makes you feel more relaxed, and it can make you feel happier. On top of all of that, smiling can make you feel more confident, though smiling is perceived differently in men and women.

Jacob M. Vigil reports in Behavioral and Brain Sciences (2009) that smiling is associated with a positive effect in women. For women, "smiling signals warmth, which attracts fewer and more intimate relationships." You'll see in the next section that when it comes to relationships, it's better to have one or two best friends than it is to have 10 acquaintances.

For men, smiling signals "confidence and lack of self-doubt." In both cases, smiling is generating confidence and happiness. For women, it's providing confidence by generating lasting relationships. For men, it's doing it just through the act of smiling. No extra work needed.

Harder Tasks

Well, we kind of knew this section was coming. Not everything in life is as easy as listening to music or wearing your lucky charm bracelet. If you really want to kick your low self-esteem out for good, you'll have to focus on some tougher tasks.

These are things that you need to consciously do all the time. They may sound easy when you first come across them, but they require more brainpower, which can be harder than running a marathon (which is also good for building self-esteem in case you were wondering).

Self-affirmations

What the heck is a "self-affirmation"? Well, it's pretty much the same as all of those other "self-something" words. Self-affirmation means that you recognize your value. If you've been through something really difficult, or if you don't love a part (or all) of your outside self, it can be really challenging to use self-affirmations.

So, how do you go about affirming yourself? Any act that demonstrates that you are worth something accomplishes this. That time you scored the winning basket at the end of the game? That was an act of self-affirmation. Any kind of accomplishment is going to be an act of self-affirmation.

However, these accomplishments don't have to be huge; they can be really small things. The thing about self-affirmations is that they often come from other people. Your teacher told you your paper is fantastic, your friend told you she loves your lipstick color, or your mother left you a sweet note in your lunch box. These are all pretty simple things, but they aren't something that you can control.

So, here's where the problem comes in. Let's say there's this week where, for some reason, no one has done or said anything affirming. No one said your paper was great, no one complimented you, and your mom didn't even make your lunch. You may not realize it, but this can lower your self-esteem, and the worst part is, you didn't have anything to do with it.

That's where you come in. If no one else is affirming your worth, you have to learn to do it yourself. It sounds a little twisted — I'm supposed to tell myself I love my lipstick color? — but it makes more sense than you may realize.

According to an article written by Geoffrey L. Cohen and David K. Sherman (2014), researchers of psychology, there are a lot of little things we can do to affirm our worth. In their article, they give some examples of these things.

They explain: "Spending time with friends, participating in a volunteer group, or attending religious services anchor a sense of adequacy in a higher purpose. Activities that can seem like distractions can also function as self-affirmations. Shopping for status goods (Sivanathan & Pettit 2010) or updating one's Facebook page (Toma & Hancock 2013) afford culturally prescribed ways to enact competence and adequacy. For people who value science, simply donning a white lab coat can be self-affirming (see Steele 1988)."

You saw that right — doing things like updating your Facebook page or going to church can be self-affirming. Pay close attention to that last line of examples — "if you love science, just putting on a white lab coat can be self-affirming" — you'll notice that there's an emphasis on passion. If you have passion for what you do, you'll find little self-affirming things everywhere.

The challenge is finding something you're passionate about. If you love singing, simply singing in the shower can be self-affirming. If you love giving advice, listening to a friend can be self-affirming. You need to be able to affirm your worth even when other people aren't, and that takes a little bit of work.

Notice when you feel down, and make a conscious effort to do the kinds of things that make you feel valuable.

Make relationships

This idea snuggles up well with self-affirmation. In the same article by Cohen and Sherman, they talk about how important it is to have connections and relationships with other people to increase your self-confidence and general happiness.

They talk about a previous study that was done to help us understand: "When people were put in a stressful situation, such as receiving mild electric shocks, those who felt they had social support in their lives, or those who simply had the chance to see a picture of a loved one, experienced less fear, threat, and pain (e.g., Master et al. 2009; see also Cacioppo & Patrick 2008)."

If you have people to rely on, that contributes to your self-worth. In order to boost your own confidence, you need to know that you aren't alone in life. That means you need to step out of your comfort zone and make friends.

However, quality over quantity is the key. Having one close friend is better than having 10 distant acquaintances, according to Nicholas Epley and Julianna Schroeder (2014). They explain that according to recent research, "a person's overall well-being appears to be driven by the quality of connections with close others rather than the quantity of connections with more distant others."

Focus on building a connection with one or two people instead of maintaining 10 distant friendships. Your confidence will thank you.

Learn how to play the piano

This one doesn't really seem to directly correlate with self-confidence, let alone the ability to find your assertive voice. But, once again, research has taught us otherwise.

A study published in Psychology of Music (2004) found that three years of piano lessons increased the participants self-esteem: "The increase in self-esteem of the children who completed three years of piano instruction was significant while the changes in self-esteem of those who never participated in piano instruction or who dropped out of the lessons were not."

How is this possible? The researchers offered up their take on the whole thing by explaining that all of the things that come along with playing the piano helped to raise the self-esteem of the children.

They said the presence of an acoustic piano in the house was often times a luxury for the family. The children got a lot of individual attention from their piano teachers, they had opportunities to play in piano recitals in front of their family and friends, and they spent time practicing at home. The act of practicing itself means that other people are probably listening, and it also might mean that parents are watching more often. The researchers say, "Any single or combination of these multiple factors might have produced the increase in self-esteem of the children taking the lessons."

If you think about this along with all the other things we have looked at, it kind of makes sense, doesn't it? The piano playing is like an act of self-affirmation — it gives the children worth, which raises their self-esteem. When they play recitals, and people they love are watching and listening, that's also an instance of self-affirmation.

So, maybe you don't have to learn how to play the piano. Doing anything that gives you self-affirmation will have the same effect as this. In fact, one of the sources within the study said that any instrument has an impact on self-esteem: "those involved in musical activities often report that learning music makes them feel better about themselves."

Doing something as simple as joining your school's band can have a similar effect. It's a commitment, and it requires your time and effort, but in the long run, it'll be worth it.

Step out of your comfort zone

In order to get to a place where you feel comfortable telling people "no," you have to take baby steps. That means you need to get a little outside your comfort zone.

If you're already thinking about skipping to the next suggestion, wait a second. It might be simpler than you think.

A study was done in 2014 by those researchers mentioned earlier, Epley and Schroeder. Their goal was to find out if speaking to a stranger affects our happiness. Keep in mind that happiness and self-esteem are directly related. Here's how they did their study.

They asked people who commuted on trains and buses to start up a conversation with a complete stranger. Well, that was one group, but that was the focus of the study. They wanted to see if talking to a stranger affected the participants.

One of the other groups was asked to go about business as usual and the other group was asked to be completely distant (picture being on a bus with headphones on).

So, what were the results?

Almost everyone thought they'd be happier if they didn't talk to a stranger — they predicted "a more positive experience in solitude." But, they were wrong. Almost all of the participants reported having a more positive experience when they connected with a stranger.

The researchers found out that the reason these people thought they'd rather be distant is because they feel like other people don't want to connect. There's this idea that other people will be bothered if you try to talk to them. The problem is that this stops us from communicating with other people, and communication is proven to make us happier. So, what are we doing with headphones on?

Here's your key to boosting your self-esteem and confidence: step out of your comfort zone and talk to a stranger. Remember that this is about baby steps.

CASE STUDY:
JACQUI, 25 YEARS OLD

I was driving home and rear-ended someone. I knew I was going to be faced with someone that would be very upset with me, and I am not good with people who are angry with me. As I saw her step out of her car, I rolled down my window and asked her to pull over, so that we were not blocking the other people trying to turn right. She gave me a look of uneasiness, suspecting me to just drive away and just call it a hit and run. But something in her mind told her to get back into her car and trust me.

As I put my car in park, I told myself to be courageous and face the person who would be very upset with me for ruining her day. I walked up to her window as she lowered it down. Before I could even speak, her first words to me were "Are you OK?" This already took me by surprise, because I thought her first words to me would be a couple of swear words. When my shock wore off, I was able to tell her that I was fine, and asked if she was OK, too.

It was in the middle of winter, so it was a tad bit cold outside. She asked me if I would like to sit in her car while she called the police to report the accident. At first, I was hesitant, you know, with her being a stranger and all, but then I decided to risk it and sit in her car while we waited. As we sat in there, we started talking. I found out that she was on her way to a funeral (which made me feel even worse), and she found out that I was worried about my husband being worried that I wasn't home yet. We talked even more and started laughing about past car accidents we were in, and other things that were just completely random.

The whole time, she seemed so calm and collected. When the cop finally got there, we were so absorbed in our conversation that we didn't even notice. The cop walked up to my car and saw no one in there. I noticed him looking in my car so I got out of hers and told him we were both in there. He looked confused, probably wondering why we were getting along so well.

After he looked at the car, he said that there wasn't enough damage to file a report, so we just decided to call it a day. We exchanged insurance information, just in case the daylight showed some damage we couldn't see, and started to part ways. She wound up not filing anything or letting the insurance companies know we were even in an accident.

You don't have to start to step out of your comfort zone by getting in a car accident (at least we wouldn't recommend it). Start out by nodding at a stranger as you cross paths. Transition into a smile. Then, a hello. Then, when you feel comfortable, start asking "how are you today?" Before you know it, you'll be hearing the life story of a stranger, and everyone has something interesting to say.

Once you do this, you'll find that it'll be much easier to stand up for yourself to the people in your life.

Go to counseling

This can be one of the hardest things you'll need to do. If you suffer from really low self-esteem, sometimes you have to go to someone else for help you. You can't always rely on yourself to fix everything.

Studies upon studies have shown that seeking counseling has positive effects on your self-esteem. Going through therapy is a way to learn about yourself and also how to make yourself better. For many, counseling is a healing process — they talk about things they feel like they can't talk about to other people, and then they learn how to deal with them from an expert.

Hudson Valley, a college in New York, outlines some of the benefits of counseling (2016). They say that counseling can do the following:

- Improve your ability to communicate with other people
- Improve self-acceptance and self-esteem
- Give you the ability to change self-defeating behaviors/habits
- Help you to manage your emotions
- Give you relief from depression, anxiety or other mental health conditions
- Increase confidence and decision-making skills
- Help you manage stress
- Improve problem-solving and conflict resolution abilities

Not only will counseling improve your self-esteem and confidence, but you can talk to your counselor about your specific problem with saying "no" to people in your life. You can work on both the underlying issue — improving your confidence and finding your assertive voice — and the *actual* issue, whatever it might be for you.

Your school probably has a counselor that you can see, which is free. If not, you can ask your parents — their work insurance might offer a counseling service that's free to you. No matter what your specific issue is, know that talking to someone else about it can give you a huge sense of relief. You just have to take that first step.

Chapter 4

Learning to Say NO

earning how to say "no" can be difficult, but there are lots of tools and strategies that you can use to make it an easier habit. This chapter will cover the overarching strategies (how to fix the core problems), but throughout the rest of the book, there are little tips and tricks sprinkled in (you know, odds and ends). Keep on reading to get to the root of the problem, and most importantly, how to fix it.

Problem Solving

Should you say "yes," "maybe," or "no?" How do you know when to make the right decision? Getting down the basics of problem solving can help you figure that out. Tim Hicks, an expert on problem-solving and decision-making strategies gives us some steps to follow to make sure we're making the right decision.

1) Figure out the problem

What exactly is going on? For this demonstration, let's say that one of your customers at work asks to borrow your cellphone. So, the first step is to be clear on what exactly the problem is.

The customer needs a way to contact someone else.

2) Figure out what everyone wants

This is a vital step, and it often goes ignored. Get to root of the problem, and lay out what everyone actually wants. In our example, the customer is stuck on using *your* phone. You don't want the customer to use your phone, especially because it's new, and you don't want anything to happen to it.

Their suggested solution to the problem is to use your phone. However, if you get to the root of the problem, which is having a way to contact someone else, any phone would do, not just yours.

3) Come up with all possible solutions

So, what are all the options? Brainstorm and be creative.

You could find out what happened to their phone (if they have one). You could offer them the company telephone. If you wanted to go a step further, you could ask them what the problem is and offer to help.

4) Evaluate the options

Is their phone dead? How urgent is the emergency? Does your boss allow customers to use the company telephone? Is their problem something you can help solve?

Weigh all the options before making a decision.

5) Choose the solution

Make the decision based on your evaluation. Which option has the most pros and the least cons?

Let's say the woman needing a telephone just arrived at the restaurant, and she realizes she forgot her phone at home. She asks if you have a cellphone.

"Miss, do you have a cellphone I can borrow?"

You get nervous; you just picked up your new phone yesterday because you busted your last one — you don't even let your brother touch it.

"What's the problem? Maybe I can help."

This may seem like you're prying, but if she's asking to use your personal stuff, you have the right to ask. By adding the offer to help, it makes your question seem less like it's an intrusion of privacy.

"Well, I left my phone at home, and I need to call my husband to let him know that we're here. I'd like to tell him we're sitting on the patio so that he knows where to go when he gets here."

This is the root of the problem — and it turns out you have the ability to solve it.

"Ma'am, we'd be happy to take your name and let your husband know when he arrives that you're sitting outside."

You solved the problem without feeling the need to say "yes" to something that you really didn't want to say "yes" to.

Communicating and Connecting

Being able to communicate and connect with other people will help when it comes to letting them down. Here are some tips and tricks you can use to ease the blow.

Show you care

People like to feel important. When someone is getting ready to ask you that question or lay that request at your feet, one of the most important things you can do is to show that you care.

Be sincere with your response, throw in a nice word or two about the person, but most importantly, listen to what they have to say. Dr. Robert Anthony, author of *The Ultimate Secrets of Total Self-Confidence* (2008) explains, "Notice that when you are talking most people can't wait for a pause so that they can begin talking. They really don't hear you. They are too busy rehearsing what they are going to say next."

We, as humans, simply like to talk, and most of the time, we like to talk about ourselves. Be aware of this human trait, and throw it under the rug when someone is asking you for something.

Don't cut them off; instead, listen intently to their whole request. Don't spend your time rehearsing your "no" while they're speaking. They'll appreciate the fact that you listened, and they will better receive your response.

The "Pregnant Pause"

Researchers Sara Bogels, Kobin H. Kendrick, and Stephen C. Levinson did a huge study on what it means when we pause before saying "yes" or "no" to someone in a conversation.

In this study (2015), they found that when you pause, people often associate the pause with low self-esteem and lying. The faster you responded, the more likely the person would be to think you were telling the truth.

So, no matter what you say, people can basically tell what you're thinking. The study showed that if you pause before answering, people assume that you want to say "no," even if you end up saying "yes."

What does this mean for you?

If an acquaintance asks you something and you pause before answering, they automatically assume you don't want to do it: "listeners anticipate a response already before it occurs," the researchers say.

Be aware of how people are interpreting your actions. If you actually want to say "yes" to someone, don't hesitate. They'll get the wrong impression.

If you want to say "no," but are finding it difficult, it's OK to pause. That will signal to the listener that you are hesitating. It might be a good idea to explain what's holding you back, since the listener already has the idea that you want to say "no."

Know the pregnant pause, and use it to your advantage.

Body language

If you're going to find your assertive voice, your body language better match it. In fact, body language is read into and believed more than what's coming out of your mouth. That means that if your words are saying "no," but your body looks weak and uncertain, that person will continue to come back to you in attempts to change your mind.

Studies have shown that 93 percent of a person's communication is through body language and nonverbal communication. Let's take a look at the different kinds of body language and how we can use those to show that we mean it when we say "no."

Eye contact

First, make and maintain eye contact. There is nothing that says, "I am sure of what I am saying" more than eye contact. Maintaining eye contact also shows that you respect the person you're talking to and that you're interested in what they're saying to you (even if you aren't).

If you start looking around while holding a conversation with somebody, it makes you look like you couldn't care less about what they're saying. The person who is constantly checking their phone, looking at their watch, or looking around the room while in a conversation gives the impression that they have something better to do or somewhere else to be. Also, the person who looks down while holding a conversation with somebody else gives off the impression of being shy, withdrawn, or even deceitful.

Be sure of yourself. When your brother asks you to watch his dog, look him in the eye when you let him down.

Distance

The distance that you keep between you and the person you are speaking with has a significant impact on how the other person may perceive you.

For instance, if you stand too far from the person, they may perceive you as standoffish. However, if you stand too close, the other person may perceive you as pushy or aggressive.

If you lean toward the person or a group of people, more than likely, they will see you as a friendly individual. On the other hand, if you lean away from people as you are holding a conversation, they may see you as unfriendly and distant.

Posture

The way you stand says a lot about how you really feel.

Here are some tips on posture that projects an assertive attitude:

- Maintain a straight back and hold shoulders back.

- Hold your head up high at all times.

- Keep your hands down by your sides. Do not put your hands around your back as this projects a timid and insecure image. Do not cross your arms, as this may come across as not wanting to listen or being defensive.

- Keep your feet flat on the ground; now is not the time to sway from your tippy toes to your heels.

Be assertive, but not aggressive

Has anyone ever cut you in line? How did you react? If you felt awkward and didn't say anything, you need to work on being assertive. If you freaked out and said something like "Uh, hello! I'm right here," you need to work on toning down the aggression. However, if you're somewhere in the middle, you probably responded like this: "Excuse me. I guess you did not see me, but I was in line first. Can you please step back?"

An assertive person is respected and even admired, but an aggressive person does not gain anyone's respect and is avoided (if possible). Unfortunately, there seems to be the misconception that if you are more forceful than you used to be, you might have become aggressive.

There is a big difference between being assertive and being aggressive. For instance, assertive people can state their opinion and remain respectful of others. Aggressive people ignore and sometimes attack other people's opinions in an effort to make their opinions seem to be the correct one.

In the following example, the individual was able to assert himself and say "no" without being aggressive.

Jason finally saved enough money to buy a used vehicle less than 2 years old with low mileage. As he worked his way through various used car dealers, he was able look around, make price comparisons, and evaluate financing options.

After spending considerable time in a large, used car dealership, he narrowed down his choice to two cars. Both were last year's models, had about the same amount of mileage, but one cost considerably more than the other. Upon making his decision to buy the one that cost the least, he found himself dealing with a salesman who insisted on his buying the more expensive model.

Jason knew he had to be firm and assertive if he was going be able to finalize the purchase without being there all afternoon arguing with the salesman. So, Jason finally looked at the salesman in the eyes, planted his feet flat on the ground, and said to him, "I appreciate you looking out for my interests, but I will not buy the more expensive vehicle. I am here to purchase the less expensive vehicle. If you cannot help me with this transaction, I am sure there are other sales representatives in the dealership who will be glad to assist me."

The sales associate was more than happy to sell Jason the cheaper vehicle.

As you can see, Jason was not aggressive or rude. He was assertive in his body language and verbal expression. He looked at the salesman in the eyes, assumed an assertive posture, and got straight to the point.

A comparison of assertive behavior versus aggressive behavior may serve as a good guideline of how to conduct yourself in different circumstances so that you project the appropriate behavior.

Assertive Behavior	Aggressive Behavior
Speaks openly	Interrupts and talks over other people
Speaks with an adequate tone of voice	Speaks louder than the others
Makes eye contact and maintains it	Stares at the other person
Stands with a relaxed but assertive posture	Stands very rigidly during conversations
Participates in group conversation	Takes control of conversations
Values other people as well as him or herself	Values him or herself more than other people
Speaks to the point	Only takes him or herself into consideration
Tries to be fair and not hurt anyone	Hurts people to avoid being hurt
Sets and reaches goals while being fair to others	Hurts others in the process of reaching goals

Winston Churchill once said, "Attitude is a little thing that makes a big difference." Your success in becoming a more assertive person and being able to say "no" has a lot to do with your attitude.

Remember that attitude is something you are in full control of. You can choose to let people run you down and make you feel like you are incapable of accomplishing anything, or you can have a positive attitude.

Be confident that the world is yours for the taking, and that you can do anything. As long as you have this attitude in the back of your head, you will have no problem finding your confident voice.

Compromise

Proposing an alternative to what is being asked of you not only eases the jolt of having said "no," but it also keeps the doors open for a positive relationship between both you and the requester.

The alternative proposed may not be exactly what everyone wants, but it closes the gap significantly. The problem with a straight up "no" is that it frustrates the person who asked, because it makes him or her feel powerless. By compromising, you're not only showing that you're easy to work with, but you're giving that person some power back.

An interesting thing about compromise is that people who have a hard time doing it don't need support to compromise — they need support to resist (saying "no"). According to David Bedrick J.D., Dipl. PW, it's hard to make compromises if the other person rarely follows through (2013). He explains using the example of compromising on a meeting time:

> "If you have always been willing to make reasonable compromises but I have regularly failed to carry out our agreed times to meet, then you have a good reason to not go along with the resolution. In addition, if I am

regularly not following through on our agreements, I too may have good reasons to not go along with the compromised agreements."

You have to put yourself in the other person's shoes. Maybe they're having a hard time compromising because they're so busy doing extra projects that they don't have time for.

In this specific scenario, that means that both parties need to agree to resist compromise. Bedrick explains, "Going further to resolve this conflict would mean helping me not agree so readily to meet at times that don't really work for me and helping you be less agreeable to meeting times when you are not convinced I will show up on time."

Here are four examples of situations where you can say "no" to the request, but still provide the person who asked with an alternative solution that will more than likely take care of the request.

1) Your out-of-town friend calls you and tells you that he is coming to visit for a couple of days, and he is bringing his yellow Labrador retriever, Diesel, with him. Your parents do not allow large dogs in your house, so you tell him that you do not have a problem with him coming to visit, but you hope he does not mind you making arrangements with the nearby dog kennel so that Diesel can stay there during his stay at your house.

2) Your friend from middle school who is in boarding school calls you and asks if it would be possible for you to pick her up at the airport Thanksgiving morning because she wants to surprise her parents. The airport

is an hour away and going to pick her up will conflict with your Thanksgiving plans, because you are having Thanksgiving at two different households. So, you tell her that you cannot pick her up because of commitments with family but you will be glad to suggest a couple of mutual friends or a taxi service who can pick her up.

3) During summer vacation, your uncle asks you to house-sit for him over the weekend while he goes on a hunting trip out of state. You tell him that you cannot house-sit for him because you have already made plans to go camping with friends. However, you suggest he check with your sister who is always looking for ways to stay busy during summer vacation.

4) Your co-worker asks you to work for her on Tuesday night. You tell her that you don't want to work any more hours than you already do, because schoolwork is becoming hard to finish. You tell her you will work her Tuesday night if she works your Thursday night.

If you propose an alternative solution when you say "no," it shows that you have given the request some thought rather than discarding it completely. The show of good will and care always goes a long way in softening a "no" response.

Chapter 5

Saying No to Friends

True friends are there for you when you need them, just like how you're there when they need you. Sometimes friends play an even bigger role in your life than your own family (don't tell Mom we said that). When things get tough, it makes a big difference to have friends to lean on.

That's why it's so difficult to say "no" to friends whenever they ask something of you. Regardless of how significant or insignificant their request may be or how capable or incapable you may be of doing it, there's always the guilt factor.

You can't help but feel compelled to agree to complete their requests because they're your friends — it feels like they're counting on you. It's also important to realize that because they are your friends, they should understand that you can't always say "yes."

Sometimes, we feel the need to please everyone by accepting invitations to tons of time-consuming events. Let's take a look at Wesley's story.

CASE STUDY: WESLEY; FULL-TIME STUDENT AND STUDENT OFFICE ASSISTANT AT THE UNIVERSITY OF FLORIDA

As a full-time student and part-time employee at the University of Florida, Wesley Baker keeps a very busy schedule. Not only does he make the time to go to school and work, but he also tries to keep in touch with his friends and family. Being a people person, he wants to be everywhere for everybody, saying "yes" more often than he should. His pattern of agreeing to things often leads to conflicts of interest with things that he should be doing.

The problem, according to Baker, is that although, on occasion, he takes time to consider the request before answering, he still agrees and ends up stretching himself too thin.

He ends up stressed out, upset, and sometimes he doesn't even enjoy the events to the fullest, because he's constantly checking his watch to see when he has to be on his way to the next one. Even though he puts in so much effort to please everyone, people are still upset because he often can't stay in any one event from beginning to end, as he has to be on his way to another one.

He wants people to feel that they can come to him when they need something, and he will be there for them. He says, "I truly stick by my friends and family, and if they ever need anything, I'll help, even if it means missing out on something I wanted to do. I have always been driven to help people and be there for them when they need me." He admits that his desire to help people has made it very difficult for him to be able to say "no" so far.

Maybe there's been a time when you've asked something of a friend, and they couldn't help you. Were you understanding of their decline? More than likely, you were. Because of the friendship that exists between you and your friends, you can be certain that if they could have been there for you, they would have.

When you have to tell a friend "no," remind him or her just how important he or she is to you. There are times when the friend is full of self-pity and in need of constant reassurance, and those "no's" need to be a little more empathetic to meet your friend's needs. The last thing you want is to lose a friendship over an unnecessarily harsh "no."

You know your friends better than anyone else, and in any long-term friendship, there will always be plenty of situations when you will have to tell each other "no." However, in a long and happy friendship, it's important to know each individual's needs, and you need to express those "no's" accordingly.

If your friend doesn't understand and gets angry with you, there are two things you can take away from it. One, they're dealing with something else that's causing them to lash out at you. Try to see things from their perspective and consider offering a more detailed explanation for why you're saying "no." Two, they're not that good of a friend. Maybe you don't want a person like that in your life. Consider slowly breaking things off.

Are they really friends or are they using you?

There are people out there who pretend to be your friends, but in reality, they're just using you to get what they want. These are the people who are around you for convenience, and although they may not be in touch constantly, they remain in touch often enough to make it seem like they really care. They constantly need something from you, and it might be because you're always saying "yes."

These are people who call you on Monday and ask how your weekend went, make small talk, and then end the conversation. Then, they call you again on Thursday and ask you if they can borrow your new dress over the weekend if you aren't going to be using it, or they ask to borrow that new video game you stood in line for hours to get.

The next week, they might call for a few minutes to tell you they were thinking about you and wondering how you were doing, but that's only because a few days later, they are going to call to see if they can come over to borrow your bike.

These are just a couple of examples of friends that are using you. They aren't going to call you and invite you over on the weekend or offer to come help you with your homework. They're obviously in the "friendship" for their benefit. There is no give and take in this situation. It's all about them and what they can get out of you.

Sometimes, it takes a while to realize that a person is taking advantage of you, but once you figure it out, you have to find that assertive voice of yours.

There are also those friends who like to use you for their own self-esteem. They are supposed to be your friends, but they use you every chance they get to make themselves look and feel better in front of others. For instance, one friend might openly talk about how you know each other from middle school and how you stayed friends through high school despite the fact that you didn't make it into the private high school like he did.

Obviously, he's using you to make him look better. His underlying message is that he was way smarter and more talented than you, because a school didn't accept you but accepted him. In other words, he might be your friend, but you are not as good as he is.

Others might make constant comments about your height or lack thereof. They are the first ones to push you to the front in group pictures or make comments about how short people can't gain a lot of weight or it shows. They say they can say stuff like that because you're friends, and you should know that they don't mean anything by it.

The truth is that you know they do mean what they're saying, but they're cowards hiding behind the veil of friendship to make themselves look better at your expense. The solution to this situation and the way to put an end to it is by saying "no" to all of it.

Regardless of how much you hate this kind of behavior, your nonverbal response allows them to keep doing it. You can say "no" to all of this by saying things like:

- "I thought you were my friend; friends don't treat friends like that."

- "I'm tired of your mean comments; you need to stop."

- "Your comments about my height are really starting to hurt my feelings."

- "I know you think it's funny, but I don't appreciate being made fun of."

Another option will depend on how you usually respond. If you're generally uncomfortable and find that you laugh with your friend because you don't know what else to do, consider showing your feelings instead.

Here's an example: You're watching a movie in history class. There's this scene where there's a small alley and your friend says, "Bet you couldn't fit in that!"

Your friends laugh, and usually, you'd probably laugh too, but this time, you look down at the ground and give a slight frown. You look genuinely hurt by the comment.

Suddenly, your friend realizes that what used to be a joke isn't actually funny anymore. This kind of response from you might be easier or more comfortable than actually speaking up. However, if this response isn't working, you do need to step out of your comfort zone and make it clear that your feelings are being hurt.

When dealing with people like this, not only do you have to learn how to say "no" to their requests and their hurtful actions, but you need to consider if they're a friend worth keeping. Having fake friends will only drain you, both physically and mentally. You get so frustrated with them that you spend precious energy being mad at them and thinking of ways to get rid of them, aside from all the time and effort you might have already invested in taking care of some of their requests.

Taking care of yourself should always be your first priority.

Preserving your friend's feelings

You know you have true friends when they worry more about saving and nurturing your relationship than resenting you for saying "no" to them. You are always going to have some give and take when it comes to asking friends for something — that's kind of what friends are for, right? You want someone you can count on and someone that is going to help and support you. However, it's important that you and your friends know that your friendship goes beyond just doing favors for each other. You need to trust each other, and there definitely needs to be some give and take.

Normally, good friends know you well enough to know that when you say "no" to a plea for something, it's for a good reason. They will understand and move on. Some may ask for an explanation, probably out of concern, while others may not even feel the need to ask.

A true friend will probably ask out of concern and will completely understand if your reason is that is you have too much on your plate. They may even try to help instead of wasting time trying to convince you otherwise. It's a lot better for you to be honest with your friends rather than trying to squeeze whatever it is in your schedule and then becoming bitter and passive-aggressive about it down the road.

Between true friends, there is an unspoken understanding that in times of need, you will do everything possible to be there for each other, whatever the case may be (that means saying "yes" sometimes). There is also the understanding that there may be times when, regardless of how badly you want to be there for them, you are just not able to do it.

Sometimes, friends just want to give you their opinion on things. For Rev. Vickie Haren, it got the point where she had to step in and say "no."

CASE STUDY:
REV. VICKIE HAREN;
CERTIFIED SPIRITUAL
LIFE COACH

Until recent years, the Rev. Haren was conditioned to say "yes" to everything since she was a child. She explains, "I was born the oldest daughter in my family. My 'job' was to take care of the house when my mother was away at work. The harder I worked, the more praise I received. I was hooked on what others thought of me, and their praise gave me wonderful energy."

In the past, the word "no" was not in the Rev. Haren's vocabulary. She could do it all and loved it when people would comment on how much work she could handle, which was a reflection of her upbringing. Then, she began to understand how she was losing herself in the process and could feel inner tension when she did not succeed in doing all she had promised to do.

This tension resulted in tremendous stress, which she noticed was having an effect on her body, her shoulders, and her neck. So, she began to pay more attention to her body, specifically how it felt in any given situation.

One of her earliest recollections of having to learn to say "no" goes back several years ago to when she owned a small manufacturing business in Ohio. She employed several women, most of whom were her friends. Each of these friends had an opinion on how to improve her business, and rather than saying "yes" to some and "no" to others, she found herself going crazy trying to implement all of their ideas.

It was at that moment that she understood she was going to have to say "no" to someone, so she decided to do what she thought would be best for her business rather than doing what everyone else was suggesting.

Now, taking time to consider the request being made of her before answering has allowed her to feel more comfortable with her final decisions. She explains, "I can't give away what I don't have."

Covering for a friend

Your friend did something bad — possibly very bad — and they want you to cover for them. This scenario happens all the time, and it puts you in a pretty awkward position. It's in your best interest to say "no" (especially if what they did is illegal).

There are a lot of things that can fall into this awkward scenario: your friend stole something, they bought or sold drugs, they vandalized something, or anything else that a friend might have done that you know was wrong.

In the moment, it's easy to give in and say that you'll cover for a friend. You need to take a step back and put things into perspective. It's easy to realize that it's not worth the risk of facing the legal consequences of your friend's actions. Know that having your friend upset with you for a little while is better than spending thousands of dollars in possible fines and court fees as well as having a record and maybe even going to jail.

If they really are your friends, they *will* realize that you did it for their own good as well as your own, and they'll forgive you. If they don't, is that really someone you want to consider a friend?

What if what they did isn't that bad? Let's say your friend is late to work, and you clock them in before they're there, or they call in sick when they're really fine, and you back them up.

You're going to be torn. It's easier to tell a friend that you won't cover for them, because you don't want to end up in prison, but when there's not a whole lot on the table, it can be more difficult. Your friend will say something like "come on, man, can you cover for me?"

It's easy to give in, but you do need to step back and think about the possible consequences. What if your boss found out that you were lying and fired you? Can you stand to lose your job over covering for a friend? Maybe your friendship is far more important than your job, but even if it is, you shouldn't have to choose between the two.

A good friend will understand if you say that you can't afford the risk of losing your job. Even if they say that there's no way you'll get caught, know that more often than not, the truth comes out. Months can pass, and then one day, at the most random time, the truth comes forward, and you'll be found out.

Lending money to a friend

This is a really sticky subject — in fact, money always is. Money is what makes the world go 'round these days, so when someone asks for it, it can put you in an awkward spot.

There are times when a friend will genuinely need the money and will ask you as a last resort — this can be really difficult for people to do. Asking for money means that you're putting your own pride aside. Treat this situation with sympathy; your friend probably feels a little awkward, too.

However, there are also friends who will ask for money and have no intention of paying you back, whether they say they will or not. They may still be true friends, but are just terrible with managing their money. They're making their own personal problems your own personal problems.

In both of these situations, you need to know that loaning money can potentially ruin a friendship. If you loan money to a friend with the expectation of getting that money back, you'll feel anger and resentment as time goes by.

Your friendship will start to fizzle out, and you'll wish you just left the money out of the equation.

CASE STUDY:
JOSH, 26 YEARS OLD

My best friend, Luke, needed a car. We had a friend selling one that was cheap and somewhat cool. I bought the car for $600 for him. It took him about two years to pay me back. I was nagging at him about it all the time, and it made me mad, but overall, it didn't make me think any less of him as a friend.

He had jobs, sources of income, and plenty of chances to pay me back, but he chose to spend his money on other things. That was the most aggravating part. That alone caused a little resentment, but I always forgive and forget, and I continued to value his friendship. So, what did I learn? Don't lend friends money. They don't make paying you back a priority.

The only time you should ever loan money to a friend (or anyone for that matter) is if you are 100 percent happy about not getting that money back.

Here are three reasons why you shouldn't loan money to a friend with a few tips on how to compromise to ease the awkwardness, courtesy of Money Crashers, which has been featured on Forbes, CNN, and The Wall Street Journal.

1) Low expectations

If you lend money to someone close to you, there usually isn't a contract or anything that you both sign. It's pretty open-ended, and the expectations are low. The person you offered the money to doesn't make it a priority to pay you back, and you have no clue when to expect the repayments.

It can be really awkward to draw up paperwork for a casual loan with a friend, but making a verbal agreement can be helpful if you decide to do it. Create a timeline with a specific date that you expect to have the money back. For example, "I need this money back by Dec. 1, so if you pay me $100 a month, you'll have repaid me by then. Does $100 a month work for you?"

2) The real issue isn't being solved

If a friend is asking you for money, try to figure out why they need it. Usually, there's a bigger problem at the core of things. If they need help paying off a credit card bill, there may be a budgeting issue. If you offer them the money, you're giving them an easy way out, which isn't actually helping them.

Instead of offering to give money, offer to help make a budget. This puts you in a better situation, and it still helps your friend.

3) You might need the money

Before you give your money to a friend, consider if *you* need it. What if you lose your job or have an emergency come up? Can you afford to give money to someone else? While you may have other people to rely on, like your parents, this puts you in an awkward place. You now have to ask your family members for money, which you might have been able to avoid had you not given out a loan to a friend.

If you don't have any kind of backup available to you, tell your friend. Simply say that you don't have the money to spare right now, but ask if you can help in any other way.

The most important thing is that you ensure your relationship with your friend isn't ruined because of money. The idea that lending money to a friend will ruin the relationship isn't a foreign idea — try mentioning that to your friend if all else fails.

Say something like, "I really want to help, but I've heard some pretty terrible things about friends loaning money to friends. I don't want our relationship to be hurt by this. What can we do to make sure this doesn't happen to us?"

Peer pressure

Saying "no" to simple things can seem hard, but when you compare them to saying "no" in a peer pressure situation, maybe they're not so bad.

As you get older, you're going to feel more pressure from your friends to do things that they think are "cool." You will start to feel pressured to drink, smoke, do drugs, have sex, and a myriad of other things that teens your age like to experiment with.

It can be really difficult to say "no" to people in these instances. They might label you the "innocent" or "wimpy" one, but it's important to know who you are. Don't do something just because other people are pressuring you to do it.

If you decide you do want to do something that people are pressuring you to do, you also need to remember the law. If friends want you to try an illegal drug, not only should you consider your own personal safety, but you should also consider what kinds of legal action could be taken against you. What's more important — impressing your friends or staying out of prison?

If your friends make fun of you for not giving in, it's safe to say that you don't want to be friends with them.

A problem that's becoming worse as we enter the age of cell-phones and technology is nude photography. When you enter into your first relationship, you may feel pressured to send inappropriate pictures to your significant other.

Aside from the severe emotional trauma you'll experience if your ex decides to post these pictures after a breakup, it's illegal if you're under the age of 18.

So, even if you feel pressured to do something you might not want to do, be aware of not only your own morals and safety, but of the law.

Jail time speaks. It kind of yells, actually.

Chapter 6

Saying No to Family

The concept of saying "no" to a loved one is the same as saying "no" to friends, but it's actually harder. Family members expect you to help them when they need you, because you're family. You feel an obligation to go out of your way at all times and at any expense, because they're family.

You may be programmed to say "yes" at every occasion, so saying "no" may feel like it isn't an option. Your family may be shocked if you deny them a request. However, you have the right to change, especially if you've reached your limits.

Saying "no" to a parent can be especially difficult, because they raised you — you kind of feel like you owe them.

You should only say "no" if you have a real reason — your family should be able to rely on you in difficult times. You'll want to be able to justify your reasoning with your family.

Is your no justified?

If you have a valid reason for saying "no," it'll be a lot easier to actually say it.

For example, your dad has asked you to help him put together the new entertainment center he just ordered. You start picturing images of manuals, hardware, and that angry smile your father gets when he becomes impatient.

If you have nothing else going on, but you decide to say "no" because it sounds like an unpleasant time, it's going to be difficult to explain that to your father. In fact, you do have an obligation to help him, especially because he's family.

However, let's say you're the key player in your coed softball team. They need you there for today's game, but your dad thinks that softball is a waste of time. He needs you *now*. You need to stand up for yourself and explain why you're saying "no." Explain that your team relies on you and that you take the game seriously. Apologize for not being able to help, but offer to come by when the game is over.

Make sure you're not making excuses; odds are you'll get tangled up in them. Parents have a way of unraveling them — be aware that whatever excuse you come up with, they will probably have a solution for it.

Lending money to family

According to American Consumer Credit Counseling, 93 percent of young Americans would lend money to a family member in need. So, if most of us are willing to lend money to family, we need to know how to do it the right way in order to preserve the relationship.

Here are some tips and tricks from Forbes:

1) Lend only what you can afford to lose

If you treat the loan like a gift, you won't feel the anger and resentment that lending money can create. Have the mindset that you won't see the money back in order to preserve your relationship.

2) Charge interest

This can feel really awkward, but it's kind of necessary if you plan on handing out a bigger loan (if someone is asking for $20, hold off on the interest). If you don't charge interest, the IRS considers your loan a "gift," which is subject to additional taxing. Use the minimum interest rate set by the IRS as a guideline. This is published every month at **https:// apps.irs.gov/app/picklist/list/ federalRates.html**.

3) Put it in writing

This is another potentially awkward situation, but if the borrower is serious about paying you back, they should have no problem with putting it in writing. It's better to be overly cautious than to be upset down the road because you didn't get your money back (keep tip No. 1 in mind).

When you put it in writing, you should include the following: how much the loan is, the timeline for repaying the loan, a schedule for repayment (how often payments are made), and what happens if the loan isn't paid back.

This clears up any possible miscommunications, and you can tell the borrower that that's your goal. Say something like, "I know money has the power to ruin relationships, and I don't want that to happen to us; let's make a written agreement to avoid any possible confusion or problems."

Make sure that both of you sign the agreement, and run by a bank to get it notarized.

Whatever you decide to do, be sure that you aren't giving away money that you don't have. Always have the mindset that you won't get the money back to avoid becoming bitter toward people you love.

CASE STUDY:
OLIVIA, 20 YEARS OLD

Olivia and her sister went to Hawaii together when they were on spring break. They had decided to split everything down the middle, but in order to book the reservations for their hotel, one of them had to put the charges on a credit card.

Olivia and her sister kept putting it off and putting it off until someone had to take initiative, or the hotel room might not be available. So, being the one who usually takes charge, Olivia went ahead and booked the hotel room for four nights.

"I knew that if I didn't go ahead and book it, it wouldn't get done," she says.

Olivia emailed the bill to her sister and let her know that she could just send a check for her half. She didn't get a response.

They met up at the airport, and Olivia didn't want to make things awkward or less fun by bringing up the cost of the hotel room, so she waited.

When they landed and got to the hotel, Olivia felt like it was the right time. She said to her sister, "Hey, I went ahead and booked the hotel on my credit card. Do you have your checkbook with you?"

"I know you did, Liv," her sister said, "I'm not stupid."

Her sister reached through her purse, and to no one's surprise, she left her checkbook at home.

They went through the trip, and Olivia started to feel resentful toward her sister, and it made her time there with her tinged with anger.

They went their separate ways, and Olivia didn't want to bring it up a third time, but she did. "Hey, don't forget about the hotel room."

"Geez, I know. I'll send you a check," her sister said.

Olivia says that to this day she has yet to receive a check. "I don't want to keep saying something; I feel like I'm being a nag."

Lending your time to family

Your cousin is having her half-birthday party again. Your sister needs your help with her bake sale. Your mom and dad ask you to babysit your baby brother (who's teething) *again*.

Everyone needs something from you, and you barely have time to finish your homework, let alone relax. You have the right to say "no," or at least offer a compromise, in situations where people are asking for your time.

First, figure out if there is someone else you know who can step in. For example, your sister needs help with the bake sale. Ask her who else is doing the bake sale, and see if they want to meet up and bake together.

Your best friend loves babies — ask her if she wants to come over that night to help you.

When actually responding to your family, let them know that you wish you could help, "I'm sorry for disappointing you, but I'm really overwhelmed with school work right now. Can we brainstorm who else might be able to help?"

As far as that half-birthday party goes, explain that you had a lot of fun last time, but you can't fit another thing into your busy schedule this time. This makes your response sound less like a "I really don't want to go to your birthday party; I'd rather take that time to relax and catch up on my Netflix," and more like a "I'm stressed out right now and am feeling a little overwhelmed."

Everyone understands that we only have so much time in the day. When you're honest and let people know that you're feeling overwhelmed by your crazy schedule, chances are that they've felt that way at one point, too.

Saying no because you really want to

Sometimes, it's not that someone needs something from you like your time or your money. Sometimes, you just really want to say "no."

Your mom wants to plan your 16th birthday party for you, but you've already started a scrapbook of ideas.

Your dad wants to teach you how to play guitar, but you couldn't care less.

If someone asks to do something for you, and you really don't want it, you shouldn't feel guilty about saying "no."

Always be appreciative in your response. Let the other person know that you're flattered that they thought of you: "Wow, what a nice offer, mom. I have this scrapbook of ideas already started. Can I show you what I had in mind?"

That lets your mother know that you love and care about her, but it also redirects the conversation and lets her know that you clearly want to plan your own party.

As far as learning guitar goes, you can give it a shot and see how you like it. If you'd rather throw up then touch that vintage guitar, speak up: "Thank you so much for offering, Dad. I wish I was interested in learning how to play guitar, but I'm just not. Can we go fishing instead?"

Chances are your dad was just looking for a way to connect with you. If you give him another opportunity to do that, he won't feel rejected by you, and you won't have to learn how to do something you don't want to. Score *and* score.

Chapter 7

Saying No in a Relationship

Saying "no" to a boyfriend or girlfriend may come more naturally to you; a relationship is all about give and take, and there should already be a mutual understanding and a sense of trust between the two of you. Saying "no" shouldn't be about getting the upper hand or showing that you have power — it should be about knowing your limits and expressing when they're reached.

Too many "no's" from either partner said in the wrong way can easily create a very hostile environment, and that's the last thing you want in a relationship. You want to be able to have your voice heard and say "no" when you need to without feeling that the other person will hold it against you.

Science shows that positive and negative responses need to have a ratio of five to one. That means that for every five positive responses, you should be able to give a negative one once. Once that ratio starts to tip down, and you're giving, say, two positive responses and three negative ones, the relationship will be bitter. Your partner will start to think that you're being selfish and that you aren't willing to compromise on anything.

However, if it starts tipping up, it means that you aren't speaking up about your boundaries. If you say "yes" to everything your partner wants, the relationship starts to become uneven, and a power dynamic will begin to form.

It's flat-out hard to say "no." Neuroscientist John D. Cacioppo explains to Pat LaDouceur Ph.D. that our brains are more sensitive to negative responses than positive ones. He says that "the brain increases its electrical output in response to negative information."

So, when you feel hurt by a denied request or a boundary that's set up, realize that it's just your brain freaking out on you — that's the stuff of a healthy relationship.

Three basic steps

Before we get into specifics (like pressuring you and dealing with their family), we should figure out what the basic steps of saying "no" in a relationship are. They're really easy, and as long as you follow these steps, your "no" will demonstrate love and respect without making your partner feel bad.

According to LaDouceur, the main steps are acknowledging the wish, making a clear statement, and saying something positive.

1) Acknowledge the wish

When you acknowledge the wish, the first thing you should say should be about the wish itself. LaDouceur gives some examples that we'll use for all three steps.

a) "I know you grew up with dogs, and you've probably been wanting a dog for a long time."

b) "You've put a lot of work into that dinner party you're holding on Saturday."

That's it for the first step — all you have to do is acknowledge their wish. For example **a**, someone wants a dog. For example **b**, someone's asking you to help him or her set up a dinner party.

2) Make a clear statement

What now? You've acknowledged their wish super politely. Now, it's time to be clear and direct. No dilly-dallying around with hints, apologies, or questions.

a) "… but I really don't want to get a dog at this time."

b) "… but unfortunately, I won't be around that morning to help."

That's it. Don't be all "I'm sorry, but I can't" or "I'm not sure I'll have time." Be clear.

3) Say something positive

The final step to making sure the other person doesn't hate you forever? (Just kidding — they won't hate you, but this will ease the pain.) Say something nice to them once you hit them over the head with the big rejection.

a) "I'd be happy to talk about it again in a year or two."

b) "Would you like to spend a few minutes talking about where you might streamline a bit?"

The first response keeps you open-minded (you never know when you might change your mind), and the second response still offers up some of your help without infringing on your Saturday morning.

That's it. Seriously.

Here's the professional, well-said, final result.

a) "I know you grew up with dogs, and you've probably been wanting a dog for a long time, but I really don't want to get a dog at this time. I'd be happy to talk about it again in a year or two."

b) "You've put a lot of work into that dinner party you're holding on Saturday, but unfortunately, I won't be around that morning to help. Would you like to spend a few minutes talking about where you might streamline a bit?"

How awesome does that sound? You're polite and assertive without being mean or aggressive.

Now, let's get into the specifics.

Pressuring you

Don't be afraid to say "no" to your significant other, especially if they're pressuring you into taking steps you aren't ready for.

This could be anything from engaging sexually to making your relationship official on social media. In any relationship, you have to talk about what you're ready for and what needs to wait. Voice your concerns to your partner about moving too fast. If they truly care about you and what you want, they'll respect your choices. If you stay silent, you're giving a silent little "yes", and you may find yourself getting frustrated. Speak up and be an equal part of your relationship.

If you voice your concerns and they're still pressuring you, get out of the relationship as quickly as you can. That should be your first sign that they don't really care about you and your well-being — their first priority is about getting what they want.

Making decisions together

There are many ways of telling your girlfriend or boyfriend "no" that will stop any hard feelings. Try using the words "we" or "us" when you come across a request. There's something up-lifting and pleasing about using the word "we" rather than just "you" or "me."

By using these words that signal togetherness, both of you have ownership in the situation and become an intricate part of whatever is being discussed. For example, compare the following statements:

"I" statements	"We" statements
"I want to go see a movie."	"We should go see a movie."
"I don't want to go to that store."	"We should do something else."
"I don't have enough money to go there."	"We should save our money for another time."

Consider the following responses:

"You" statements	"We" statements
"You aren't going to the movies."	"Can we do something else tonight?"
"You're going to the store with me."	"What if we're only there for five minutes?"
"You never have enough money."	"What if we both chip in tonight?"

Every time you're in a situation where you need to make a decision, be careful to stay away from "I" and "you" statements. You and your partner are a team — make decisions together.

Decisions that involve his or her family

If you're ever in a situation where you're dealing with your boyfriend or girlfriend's family, you need to treat it with a lot of thought and consideration. You must be very tactful and thoughtful, because in such instances feelings can easily get hurt.

The last thing you want is your partner thinking you don't want to spend time with his or her family (even if you don't — you have to suck it up).

Creating a balance by interacting equally with both families is important for the overall balance that you have to have in a successful relationship.

Setting boundaries

Setting boundaries doesn't mean that you're saying "no" to your partner or your relationship — it just means that you're saying "no" to a particular idea or event. We're all different and need different things to function, so if someone is intruding in on that, you have to speak up and set boundaries.

Andrew Wald, LCSW-C, a psychotherapist who works with couples, did an interview with PsychCentral and explained what happened at the beginning of his marriage (2012): "When [we] were just newlyweds, [my] wife fell off her bike coming around a corner. [I] jumped off [my] bike and raced over to her. But before [I] could help, she put her hand up and told [me] to stay away. [I] was taken aback and felt rejected" (qtd. in Tartakovsky).

He explains that when they got to talking, he started to realize that his wife prefers to comfort herself, and she likes to be alone when she's sick — Wald is the opposite. They each try to respect each other's boundaries.

It's so important that you speak up about how you do things. If your boyfriend wants to hang out every night and you need alone time to survive life, you have to explain that. If your girlfriend wants you to take her on a date every other night, you have to explain that you don't make enough money to support that kind of lifestyle right now.

When you say "no" to your partner, it empowers you and creates a sense of trust. Your partner will know that you're being honest, and he or she will start to do the same. That's how you become comfortable and create a long-lasting relationship.

Keeping things equal

The saying "opposites attract" refers to people with different qualities coming together and filling in each other's blanks. For example, one person has a short temper but has a lot of motivation. The other person is very patient but has a hard time finishing projects. These two people can come together and help each other by offsetting their bad qualities.

If you're a giver and your partner isn't, sometimes it can feel like you're putting in all the time and effort while the other person isn't.

Voice your concerns; next time your girlfriend asks you to pick up takeout for her, ask her if she'd be willing to pick it up next time. If your boyfriend asks you to go to his family event, ask if he'll go to yours next time.

The most important thing is that there's give and take in the relationship. If you're constantly saying "yes" and your partner is constantly saying "no," make sure you talk about it, and keep things equal.

Saying No at Work and School

S aying "no" to your co-workers, your boss, your classmates, and your teachers is a completely different situation than saying "no" to people that are close to you like your family and friends. Saying "no" doesn't always involve actually saying the word "no." It can also be not accepting a situation, a request, or even a comment, which at times can be a double-edged sword. Depending on how it's said, people might think of you as a person who doesn't want to give more than what's required.

Not only can you be perceived as "the lazy one" or the one who isn't willing to go above and beyond, but people can also look at you as stuffy or sensitive when you say "no" to situations that make you uncomfortable. For example, when your co-workers are rude or are treating you in a way that is borderline (or actual) harassment, you have the right to say "no" to it.

So, why do we feel the need to constantly say "yes" to to our co-workers, classmates, bosses, and teachers?

Harmony Stalter, author of the book, *Employee Body Language Revealed: How to Predict Behavior in the Workplace by Reading and Understanding Body Language*, gives us three reasons:

1) **Groupthink:** People go along with whatever the majority of the group agrees to rather than stating their feelings on the matter. By agreeing with the majority, the person avoids being set aside as the outcast for not agreeing and avoids any confrontation with the remainder of the group for differing in opinions.

2) **Fear of standing alone:** Nobody wants to be looked at as the uncooperative person who doubts the boss or teacher's capabilities by not agreeing with him. Therefore, employees and students just agree with what the boss or teacher has to say to avoid the possible repercussions.

3) **Indifference:** This is when someone has lost so much interest that he or she becomes indifferent and simply agrees to things. It's very possible that this indifference

is a result of trying to make a difference in the past and having been ignored.

All of these are just ways of getting by at work — you need to stand up for yourself and learn how to say "no."

When your boss or teacher doesn't take no for an answer

Some adults just don't know how to take "no" for an answer. They believe that they got to their position through hard work, so they expect that same amount of hard work from you without caring to understand your personal situation.

When you find yourself in a situation where you feel that your boss or teacher just doesn't know how to take "no" for an answer, take a moment to evaluate the situation before you continue to accept what is going on.

So, can you say "no" to them? Absolutely, as long as it is appropriate and is done respectfully. Also, don't forget that many bosses and teachers have a boss of their own, and in situations where you have negotiated as best as possible, you can always consider going to the next level of authority.

Be ready to compromise. Compromising can provide you with the ammunition you need in future battles — "The last time you asked me to work on Easter, I did, as long as I could have Thanksgiving off. Why did you schedule me on Thanksgiving when we made a compromise?"

Be firm and don't make excuses. When you make excuses, you will sound weak to people who have a solution or answer to each of those excuses, leaving you no room to get out of their request.

CASE STUDY: SKYLYNN, 18 YEARS OLD

"Before going on our choir tour, our choir director got all of the seniors together and asked if we could do devotions on the bus. When no one said anything, she pulled the card that 'you're seniors; you should step up,' which made us feel like we had to. We didn't really have much of a say. It's like she had the idea that we're lazy and we don't care.

It's like because we're seniors, we're supposed to be leaders, but not everyone's personalities are like that. We show that in different ways."

Depending on what kind of job you have, you may be assigned different tasks or projects. If you really want to impress your boss or your teacher with your work, learn how to say "no" when you are being asked to do too many things at once (unfortunately, this doesn't really work for homework, but you can try). They will more than likely appreciate you turning in quality work rather than a large quantity of bad work.

If the work has to be returned to you for corrections and changes because it was done halfheartedly, you'll wish you had said "no" to that extra, optional assignment. If your boss questions you, ask him which he prefers: "Would you prefer a smaller amount of quality work or a larger amount of lesser quality work?"

If your boss makes requests that do not fall within your job description, are unreasonable, or are even of a personal nature, you have every right to deny the request, but remember to do so respectfully.

Say Bruce is going out of town on vacation for a week and asks his assistant Emily to take care of a couple of projects for him while he's out. Already bogged down with extra work, Emily gets a phone call from Bruce on Thursday.

He asks her to go to his house in the morning and again in mid-afternoon to take his dogs out and feed them, because the pet sitter had an emergency. Emily is already way over her head with work and knows she only has a couple more days left in the week to accomplish all she has to do.

To avoid further burdening herself, Emily tells Bruce that there is no way she can spare the time from work to take care of his dogs, and instead, she can get him the phone number to an alternate pet sitting service that could take care of his dogs that day.

Emily needs to be assertive and not compromise her ability to complete her assigned work in order to take care of the boss's personal needs. Ultimately, Emily cannot get fired or reprimanded for not taking care of the boss's dogs, but she can get in trouble for not completing her work.

Always be polite and respectful, no matter the situation or request.

Denying requests

Saying "no" to a co-worker or classmate seems like it would be easier than saying "no" to your boss or teacher, but there's this idea that if you help them, they'll return the favor. The problem is that you might end up helping them way more than they ever help you.

It's OK to help each other in the workplace or at school, but it is another thing to be taken advantage of or to take advantage of people. Next time Kevin asks you to cover the phone for him, you need to tell him that you would, but at this moment you do not have the time to spare. Next time your classmate asks you to give her a ride home (she lives across town, and you aren't even friends), say "My mom needs me to be home for dinner. Maybe Emily can take you."

CASE STUDY:
JORDANIA, 18 YEARS OLD

"I was at volleyball practice, and after the practice there was this girl that I didn't particularly like. She's just really stuck up and ignorant. She asked me for a ride, and everyone else left, so I was the last one to leave. She asked me, because I was the only one who drove. I could've said 'no,' but I felt obligated to drive her. I didn't want to, though."

Although it's nice of you to help your co-workers and classmates, they are shining due to your help, while you are struggling to get your work done.

The same thing goes for shift requests. When Kelsey asks you to work for her on Monday night, the slowest, most boring night of the week, and you tell her "yes," don't expect her to work your crummy shift next week. If you had plans, don't be afraid to deny her the request. Explain that you have already made plans and that the next time she needs help, she needs to give you more notice.

Never expect anything in return when you help your co-workers or classmates. If you constantly take Kelsey's unwanted shifts, don't expect her to take yours. If you don't want or need the money, don't take the shift. If it's an emergency, it's great to help out, but if there seems to be an emergency every week, explain that you don't have the time to work more than you already do.

Group projects

We don't know when, but at some point you will be asked to do a group project. It's inevitable. Although they can be interesting and challenging at times, it can become a stressful situation when some members of the team don't do their share of the work.

Some do less than others, because their participation in the project doesn't require as much input, but others might just slack off because they know you'll do the extra work. Unless you have the skills and inner strength to say "no" to people who ask you to do their work for them, you are going to be in deep trouble.

If the problem lies with being asked to do more by one or more members of the team, you have to be able to say "no." You need to be straightforward, yet polite. You don't want to give them any negotiating room. For example, you can say things like:

- "I wish I could take care of that portion of the project for you, but I already have enough to do as it is."

- "I know you have a lot of work to do with this project, but I can't help you with your assignment and complete mine at the same time."

- "I'm flattered that you want me to help you with that, but I don't have time, because I still have a lot of work to do before our deadline."

If you know you have the tendency to take on more than what has been assigned to you when working on group projects, make a conscious effort to set boundaries from the very beginning. This usually happens to leaders — some people are naturally good at divvying up tasks, and they're the ones who contact everyone to set up the project. Every group needs a strong leader, but if that sounds like you, you need to be sure that you aren't getting in over your head with extra work.

Evaluate the assignment that has been given to you, and establish a deadline to get it accomplished, taking into consideration all the other work that you are responsible for in addition to the project. If you consider taking on more than what has been assigned to you, you'll end up staying up too late and using up all your free time, which you should avoid at all costs as it will only cause you unwanted stress.

Not being able to say "no" when you're working on a group project can have disastrous results, because the whole purpose of working on a project as a group will be defeated. When a group is put together to work on project, it normally includes people who bring different talents and skills to the table. When you put these people together, it teaches you how to work with different people and how to successfully complete a project.

When you take on more than your share, not only are you going to be jeopardizing the quality of your assignment, but you may also be unintentionally sabotaging the success of the project. In the end, trying to take on more than you are prepared to handle is not worth it for anybody involved.

Covering for a co-worker or classmate

Covering for anyone, include your best friend, puts you in a really weird position. You want to be on their good side, but you also don't want to get in trouble. Co-workers and classmates are especially difficult to deal with, because you probably see them more than your own family. You're going to see them whether you cover for them or not.

The other difficult thing about covering for them is when you aren't necessarily in the situation, but when you see a situation like this happening. If you see something unethical happening, and you don't say anything, you're an accomplice to the scheme.

Let's turn to Emily for her story.

CASE STUDY: EMILY, 17 YEARS OLD

Emily is one of several volunteers who work on a regular basis at one of her local church's food pantry. One day, Emily spotted Natalie, one of the regular volunteers, loading several boxes of goods in her car.

Emily asked Trevor, one of the other volunteers, why Natalie was loading things in her car. Trying not to be too obvious, Trevor quietly told Emily that Natalie has been taking goods from the pantry on a regular basis and selling them at her flea market stand. He then asked Emily not to say anything.

Emily knows it is completely unethical, not only for Natalie to be taking the goods that have been donated, but also for everybody else to cover for her. She also knows it will be unethical for her to keep quiet and be an accomplice to the scheme. Emily tells Trevor that no, she cannot keep quiet, and that she will not be part of the situation.

She has two choices: she can either side with her co-workers or speak up and have them turn their backs on her. Emily does what is right and speaks to the church officials about what has been happening, letting them handle it from there.

At the end of the day, covering for anyone just isn't worth it. You risk losing your job or potentially your grades when you do (have you ever seen someone cheat on a test or paper?). You also put your own personal ethics at risk — who are you? When you cover for someone else, you're defining who you are.

If your co-worker is doing something that's costing the company money, he will most likely be fired, and you won't have to deal with him again.

Rude behavior and harassment

If your boss or your co-workers are disrespectful or rude to you, you have to speak up — the same thing goes for classmates or teachers (we sure hope teachers aren't your biggest problem!). There are a lot of things you can do to both stop the harassment and to assert yourself. Let's turn to certified harassment adviser, Melissa Martin (2013), for some tips and tricks.

1) Write down the details

The first thing you need to do is document when it happens. Martin explains, "Keep a detailed journal of what occurred with as many details as possible. If there are witnesses, compile their names." When you write things down, especially with details (names, dates, and exactly what happened), you won't forget.

I know that sounds nuts — how could I forget what happened to me? — but the human memory is a strange thing. A recent study was done at Northwestern University on how our memory changes (2012).

When we remember things, the original memory changes a little bit because of the fact that we're remembering it (what?).

OK, here's how the study went.

The researchers asked 17 people to a look at a picture. The picture was of a scene (like a beach), and in that scene was a small object (like an apple). Then, they were shown a new picture (like a farm) with the apple in a different spot. They were asked to move the apple to its original spot in the beach picture.

Everybody got it wrong.

To go a step further, the researchers then gave the participants back the beach picture with the apple in its original spot, the second spot, and a completely new spot. They were asked to point out the original spot, but they always chose the second one.

Basically, their original memory was overwritten by the new memory (they did brain scans and everything).

The lead researcher explains what this means to NPR (2014), "Memory is not intended to allow you to remember what you did last week or to remember your childhood. The point is to help you make good choices right now."

Have you ever played the game "telephone?" One person whispers a phrase into someone else's ear — "I love coffee" — and the phrase keeps going down the line until the last person hears the phrase. Most of the time, the phrase has slightly shifted or has changed completely, because people hear the phrase a little differently — "Olive got free."

Well, it seems that our memory kind of does the same thing. Every time we remember something, that memory shifts a little bit. Each time we recall the original, it shifts, and it shifts, and it shifts, until eventually, the memory might be completely made up.

So, the point is, write down what's happening to you — if you remember the incident one way, and the person who harassed you remembers it differently, people might not take you so seriously. When you say, "I wrote down all the details the exact day it happened," it gives you some credibility, and people will realize that the situation is very serious.

2) Channel your inner optimist

OK, so that's not *exactly* what Martin said to do, but she explains that when you use your mind to purposefully think positively, it can have a huge impact on your stress level. Harassment can be really stressful, but she explains that if you change the way you think to remember that this stressful situation is temporary, you can "transform negative thoughts and energy into positive thoughts and positive energy."

She also suggests keeping a journal where you write down good things that happen to you (she calls it the Joy Journal). If you're really into organization and neatness, this might be a great tool to help you stay positive.

Keep a detailed journal with dates and everything, and write down everything good that happened to you that day. Then, when you take a step back and look at your whole day, you'll realize that that rude co-worker or that harassing boss is only a small piece of your delicious (insert favorite kind of pie here) pie.

3) Use your voice (or don't)

That advice seems a little confusing, but you should speak up for yourself depending on the situation.

If someone is harassing you, tell them it isn't acceptable. Use "I don't" phrases (which will be talked about in more detail below) such as "I don't appreciate the way you're treating me right now."

Sometimes people disguise their behavior as a joke, so when you clearly say that it isn't funny to you, other people will stop thinking of it as funny, too (that rhymed).

If someone is constantly bullying you at work, sometimes it's best to not react. Bullies thrive off of power, so when you react, you're giving it to them. That's the fuel they need to keep it going.

4) Get help

Once you've written it down and have done everything you can to stop the behavior yourself, it's time to seek some help. Go to your boss and tell her what's going on (if it feels right, now's the time to bring out that list). Your boss is the one harassing you? Go to the next person up in authority. There isn't anyone? Go to the Better Business Bureau.

To file a complaint with the BBB, visit **www.bbb.org/consumer-complaints/file-a-complaint/get-started**.

Keep in mind, though, that your complaint has to fit in with their requirements, which is "disputes that relate to marketplace issues experienced with the services or products a business provides," according to their website.

They don't handle issues like these:

- Employee/employer disputes;
- Discrimination claims;

- Matters that are/have been litigated/arbitrated;
- Complaints against individuals not engaged in business;
- Issues challenging the validity of local, state, or federal law;
- Complaints against government agencies, including the postal service;
- Matters not related to marketplace issues.

If you're dealing with those issues, you can decide to get a lawyer, or you can start applying to other places so that you can get out of the hostile environment you're in.

Strategies for saying "no" with no hard feelings

You want to say "no" without damaging your relationships with the people you work with.

Here are some simple strategies that can help you assert yourself without causing any unnecessary hard feelings, with some help from Nikelle Murphy (2016), writer and assistant editor for "The Cheat Sheet."

1) Sandwich your "no"

No, we don't mean hand out a sandwich when you have bad news (though that might actually help now that we're thinking about it).

This means that when you give someone a negative response, you frame it with two positive things. For example: "The holiday pay for Thanksgiving sounds great, but I promised my family I would be there with them. I'd be happy to come the day after."

This strategy can apply to anyone, anywhere. It's a great way to give bad news or harsh criticism to people without hurting their feelings (or at least softening the blow).

2) Listen to the whole request

If someone is asking you to do something and you know by word three that the answer is "no," don't cut them off.

Let them finish their entire request before responding. It shows respect and lets them know that you care about them and are at least considering what they're asking of you.

3) Get to the point

"Well, you see, the thing is, I just… I, uh…"

Don't let that be the beginning to your answer. Nothing is more awkward than someone standing there, knowing very well that your answer is going to be "no," but they have to stand there while you try to break it to them.

Instead of dragging out your answer because you feel guilty, try using "I" or "it" phrases instead "you" phrases. Also, use the phrase "I don't" instead of "I can't." The listener gets the feeling that things are set in stone, and that you have previously established boundaries.

"I don't" statements	"You" statements
"I don't work Sundays."	"Can you find someone else?"
"I don't work more than three days a week."	"Why can't you work?"
"I don't take on more than one project at a time."	"Can you ask someone else?"
"I don't appreciate you speaking to me that way."	"Did I do something to deserve the way you're speaking to me?"

When you compare the "I don't" statements to the ones that have "you" in them, you can tell they have a bit more *oomph*. There's a "don't mess with me" vibe going on, but it isn't in a rude way; it's more of a "I decided a long time ago that this is where I draw the line for myself; it's nothing personal" kind of thing.

4) Don't set up a trap

Do you ever find yourself starting to say, "Maybe next time," or "I don't work Sundays, but if you ever are completely desperate, I might be able to help" even if you never actually plan on saying "yes" to this particular request? Don't set up a trap for yourself.

Guess what? When you say "Maybe next time," the other person is thinking, "Oh, next time, cool."

Here you are, next time, trying to figure out how to say "no" again. You don't have to say, "No, I will never help you on this kind of project ever," or "Don't ever ask me to pick up a Sunday shift again." Just don't say that you will next time.

Give them your handy, sandwiched response, and move on.

Chapter 9

An Ongoing Plan

I f you're going to stop being a people pleaser, you
have to have an ongoing plan. There is nothing
wrong with helping people and being there for
them in times of need. However, you need to find that line
between being a helpful person and stretching yourself past what
you can handle.

You can't be there for everyone all the time. You have to make
sure that you're taken care of before you can do anything else.
Here are some things you can do to keep your confidence up in
the long run.

How to Keep Being Confident

Take a good, long look at the suggestions in Chapter 3, and go for it! The easy tasks are things you can do on a daily basis. Don't discount them — put them into practice to keep your confidence up.

Know your strengths and weaknesses. If you can identify who you are, you can move forward with building your confidence and keeping it high.

Make a list. What are my strong suits, and what do I need to work on? Celebrate your strengths, and make a point to set small, short-term goals to build up your weaknesses.

If you want to be more confident for a particular task, be prepared. Learn everything there is to know about that thing so that you can be confident going into it.

Is the basketball coach is pestering you to join the basketball team? Prepare yourself. Learn how much time you'll need to dedicate to the team, find out how interested you are, and weigh the pros and cons.

Before giving a response, do your research, and have an informed answer ready.

This is the same concept as studying for an exam. When you've studied for hours and hours (those color-coordinated flashcards included), you feel prepared and confident when it comes time for the exam. That's the same thing that will happen if you prepare yourself for everything else. If someone asks you for something, ask for a little bit of time. Use that time to prepare yourself.

Put Yourself First to Master the Assertive "No"

Remember that your first priority is taking care of yourself before you take care of other people.

When someone asks you to do something for him or her, realize that you *do* have a choice. It's always a yes or no question, and you also have the ability to compromise.

Here are some last-minute tips to help you put yourself first:

1) Ask for some time

There's no reason you should have to immediately respond to someone else's request. When you give yourself some time to think about it, you avoid realizing (after it's too late) that you wish you would've said "no."

When they ask you, simply say, "Can I get back to you on that?" or "Let me sleep on that, and I'll get back to you."

This gives you some time to decide whether you actually have the resources, whether it be time, money, or your sanity, to agree to the request.

It may not be the only answer for you, but it can definitely help you by giving you a head start. Here's April's story.

CASE STUDY: APRIL; PHARMACEUTICAL SALES REPRESENTATIVE

April Colton's typical day as a pharmaceutical sales rep starts early and usually ends late. Sometimes, she even goes out of town for work; she's a pretty busy woman. People constantly ask her for things, and she used to be bad about taking on too much. However, she says she's actually gotten better, because she realized what her problem was.

She finally figured out that the problem was her constant impulse to say "yes" on the spot. Now, she asks the person if she can get back to them at a later time before she commits. Taking the time to get back to people allows her time to figure out if the request is realistic for her.

To figure out if she should say "yes" or "no," she weighs the cost versus the reward. This is a fancy way of figuring out if the task is made worthwhile by the reward of having accomplished it. If the task will take a lot more work and effort than she can give, and she doesn't think she'll get enough out of it, she'll decline the request.

Colton explains that our brain will trick us into saying "yes" because it feels good, but then we end up getting stressed out, which cancels out all the benefits of saying "yes" in the first place. She gives us the low-down: "Giving and doing things for other people gives us all a neurochemical cocktail boost of serotonin, our 'happy-feel-good' neurotransmitter, and dopamine, another neurotransmitter, that gives us pleasure and is highly involved in the brain's reward system."

Remember that while the serotonin feels good now, it'll feel a lot worse later on when the stress hormones kick in.

2) Set limits

If someone is asking you for your time or money, set a limit. They're asking you to help out with that all-day fundraiser? Say you're only available from 12 – 1 p.m. They're asking you to make a $50 donation to the booster club? Say that you only have $10 left in your budget.

You have to ability to set limits.

3) Be respectfully assertive

That assertive voice is hiding within you, and it's begging to come out. Remember that there is a difference between being firm and being mean. Be confident in your "no," but put yourself in the other person's shoes to ease the denial.

They're asking you to babysit this weekend? Respond with, "I totally understand needing to get away. I wish I could help, but I already have plans for this weekend. I'll ask around to see if I can find someone else for you."

4) Don't go overboard with the excuses

You shouldn't feel the need to explain yourself. If you feel like "no" is the right answer, that's all you need to say. Once you start giving out the excuses, the other person will jump in and find solutions to them. Moms are especially good at this.

While it's tempting to defend your answer, it's important that you keep it to the minimum. The other person might think your need to relax is less important than their need to have you at their event.

Instead of saying, "I'm sorry I can't come to your party. I'm in some serious need for relaxation, and I was looking forward to doing absolutely nothing," try saying, "My schedule has been really hectic. I won't be able to come, but I'll be sure to send (insert name here) many birthday wishes."

5) Notice your apologies

If you're a serial people pleaser, odds are you're probably saying, "I'm sorry" way too often. Next time you find yourself apologizing, ask yourself if there's anything you should actually be apologizing for.

If you aren't at fault, stop apologizing. If your co-worker asked you to work for him, and you said, "I'm sorry, but I can't," you really don't have anything to apologize for. So don't.

6) Don't be afraid of the aftermath

You might be thinking, "Yeah, I get it. I know *how* to say "no," but what about what happens after I actually do it?"

You're worried about hurting your relationship or being looked at as the lazy, unhelpful one. Here's the thing — when you say "no" to someone, they might be slightly upset at first, but within minutes, they're already focused on who they're going to ask next.

People don't think about you as much as you might think they do. Even if you say "no" to a bigger request, like your best friend asking you to be the maid of honor or the best man in his or her wedding, it won't result in a ruined relationship. If you have an actual, genuine friend, they will understand, and they will get over it.

We all have limits when it comes to our time, our money, and our emotions. Being able to set boundaries for them and actually following through on those boundaries is the key to being able to say "no" to anyone.

Setting Goals

The most important thing in this entire book is that you set some goals. Seriously, if you forget everything in the whole book (although we sure hope you don't), make sure the one thing you do is set some goals.

All of the positive things that come from setting goals should motivate you to do it, no questions asked.

Goals give your life purpose — without goals, you'll be near retirement, plating up some fries, and asking your boss if you can use the restroom.

You stop dwelling on the small stuff. When you set a goal, you focus on the bigger picture. So, the next time you get a flat tire and you're late to that part-time job, you'll remember that this is just a small setback. It has no real lasting impact on your overall goals.

Setting goals actually gets you going. When you have a clear image of where you want to go, your brain actually motivates you to take baby steps to get there, each and every day. If you have a goal that you want to get in shape by summer, your brain will motivate you to take those steps. If you have this idea in your head that one day you'd like to be fit, it'll just be this big, black blob hanging over your head that'll never really happen.

This also reduces your stress. When you jump from one thing to another without a clear goal in mind, it stresses you out. When you focus on that one specific goal (or set of goals), you'll find that you're a happier, more positive person.

When you have goals, you'll stop wasting your time. Have you ever had a day where you just lounged around, watched TV, and didn't really do... anything? How did it make you feel?

If you've ever had a day (or a string of days) like this, you know that it makes you feel pretty useless. When you set goals, you become motivated to do things with substance, which gives you purpose.

Finally, the most important thing about setting goals (for you) is that it'll help you to say "no" to those requests that you don't want to accept.

If someone asks you to go to an event on Saturday, and your goal is to get a 4.0 GPA, you have a clearer reason for saying "no." You want to take that time to study and refresh your mind.

If someone asks you to donate supplies for the bake sale, you can say, "No, I'm saving money for college, and I don't mess with my budget so that I can reach my goals."

When you have goals, your focus is sharper. This will also help you to say "yes" when the time is right.

Your goal is to have a great résumé for when you apply to your first job? Say "yes" to that volunteering opportunity. Your goal is to give away 10 percent of what you make to charity? Say "yes" to that fundraising request. Your goal is to be closer to your mom? Say "yes" to that mother-daughter event.

When you begin to frame your life around your goals, everything starts to fall in place.

Conclusion

greeing too often to do tasks for others, taking on too many assignments, and not knowing when to say "no" are more than likely one of the reasons why you may be feeling so overwhelmed. One of these is probably the reason why you picked up this book.

Learning how to say "no" is not about saying "no" to everything and to everyone. It's about saying "no" when there's too much on your plate, when you feel like it's morally right, and when you need to stand up for yourself.

Hopefully, you don't put this book down and go on a "no" spree — you certainly shouldn't cut yourself off from every opportunity and request that comes your way. The most important thing is that you learn what you can handle and frame all of your decisions around your goals.

You have what it takes. Now go make it happen!

Appendix A

Fill Out Your Mini Joy Journal

I f you remember reading about Melissa Martin's keys to dealing with harassment and rude people in Chapter 8, you'll remember that she suggested keeping something called a Joy Journal.

The purpose of this journal is to remind yourself of all the positive things in your life, which raises your self-esteem and makes it easier for you to stand up for yourself. It's a wonderful little waterfall of goodness.

Her suggestion is to actually keep a detailed journal that you might update every night before you go to bed. To get you started, try brainstorming the things you have to be happy about. Write them down here. If it feels like a nice release, you might consider going out and purchasing a little journal to keep it going.

What good things have happened to you this year?

What good things have happened to you this week?

What good things have happened to you today?

Map Out Your Goals

 e're serious about this goal thing.

Fill out the chart below to get a clearer sense of where you are and where you want to go.

My main goal:

_____

_____

Where I am now:

_____

_____

Where I want to be in one month:

_____

_____

How to get there:

_____

_____

Where I want to be in one year:

_____

_____

How to get there:

_____

_____

Where I want to be in five years:

_____

_____

How to get there:

_____

_____

That goal should be your biggest concern right now. However, having just one goal is probably not realistic. We have tons of goals in life! Keep on going.

My main goal:

_____

_____

Where I am now:

_____

_____

Where I want to be in one month:

_____

_____

How to get there:

_____

_____

Where I want to be in one year:

_____

_____

How to get there:

_____

_____

Where I want to be in five years:

_____

_____

How to get there:

_____

_____

Push yourself, and try to fill out one more.

My main goal:

_____

_____

Where I am now:

_____

_____

Where I want to be in one month:

_____

_____

How to get there:

_____

_____

Where I want to be in one year:

_____

_____

How to get there:

_____

_____

Where I want to be in five years:

_____

_____

How to get there:

_____

_____

Glossary

Addiction: The fact or condition of being addicted to a particular substance, thing, or activity.

Anxiety: A feeling of worry, nervousness, or unease, typically about an imminent event or something with an uncertain outcome.

Assertiveness: Having or showing a confident and forceful personality.

Body language: The process of communicating nonverbally through conscious or unconscious gestures and movements.

Brusque: Abrupt or offhand in speech or manner.

Cognitive-behavioral therapy: A type of psychotherapy in which negative patterns of thought about the self and the world are challenged in order to alter unwanted behavior patterns or treat mood disorders such as depression.

Confidence: The feeling or belief that one can rely on someone or something; firm trust.

Groupthink: The practice of thinking or making decisions as a group in a way that discourages creativity or individual responsibility.

Hypersensitivity: Emotional fragility.

Hypervigilence: An enhanced state of sensory sensitivity accompanied by an exaggerated intensity of behaviors whose purpose is to detect threats.

Mental trigger: Something that sets off a memory tape or flashback.

Negative self-talk: The expression of thoughts or feelings which are counter-productive and have the effect of demotivating oneself.

OCD: Excessive thoughts (obsessions) that lead to repetitive behaviors (compulsions).

Optimist: Disposed to take a favorable view of events or conditions and to expect the most favorable outcome.

Panic attack: A sudden feeling of acute and disabling anxiety.

Passive-aggressive: Of or denoting a type of behavior or personality characterized by indirect resistance to the demands of others and an avoidance of direct confrontation, as in procrastinating, pouting, or misplacing important materials.

Peer pressure: Influence from members of one's peer group.

People pleaser: Nice and helpful person that never says "no."

Pregnant pause: A prolonged silence that happens after someone says something.

Roger Ebert (1942-2013): An American film critic and historian, journalist, screenwriter, and author. He was a film critic for the Chicago Sun-Times from 1967 until his death in 2013.

Self-affirmation: The recognition and assertion of the existence and value of one's individual self.

Self-confidence: A feeling of trust in one's abilities, qualities, and judgment.

Self-doubt: Lack of confidence in oneself and one's abilities.

Self-esteem: Confidence in one's own worth or abilities; self-respect.

Self-sabotaging: Behavior that creates problems and interferes with long-standing goals.

Social anxiety: An anxiety disorder in which a person has an excessive and unreasonable fear of social situations.

Steve Jobs (1955-2011): An American information technology entrepreneur and inventor; he was the co-founder, chairman, and CEO of Apple Inc.

Workaholic: A person who compulsively works hard and long hours.

References

"Addiction and Low Self-Esteem." *AlcoholRehab.com.* DARA Thailand, Jan. 2016. Web. 27 Mar. 2016.

"Definition of Self-Confidence." Merriam-Webster. Merriam-Webster. Web. 16 Mar. 2016.

"Depression." NIMH RSS. National Institute of Mental Health, Mar. 2016. Web. 24 Mar. 2016.

"Eating Disorders." NIMH RSS. National Institute of Mental Health, Feb. 2016. Web. 24 Mar. 2016.

"HVCC Center for Counseling - Personal & Psychological Counseling." *HVCC Center for Counseling.* Rensselaer County, 2016. Web. 18 Mar. 2016.

"Self-Confidence, n." *OED Online*. Oxford University Press, Mar. 2016. Web. 16 Mar. 2016.

"Self-Esteem Definition." *Merriam-Webster*. Merriam-Webster. Web. 16 Mar. 2016.

"Self-Esteem, n." *OED Online*. Oxford University Press, Mar. 2016. Web. 16 Mar. 2016.

"The Definition of Self-Confidence." *Dictionary.com*. Web. 16 Mar. 2016.

"The Definition of Self-Esteem." *Dictionary.com*. Web. 16 Mar. 2016.

American Consumer Credit Counseling. "More than 90 Percent of Americans Would Loan Money to a Family Member in Need." *ConsumerCredit.com*. American Consumer Credit Counseling, Inc., 14 Nov. 2013. Web. 21 Mar. 2016.

Anthony, Robert. *The Ultimate Secrets of Total Self-Confidence*. 2nd ed. New York, NY, U.S.A.: Berkley, 2008. Print.

Bedrick, David. "To Compromise or Not to Compromise." *Psychology Today*. Sussex, 3 Apr. 2013. Web. 22 Mar. 2016.

Better Business Bureau. "Online Complaint System." *Better Business Bureau*. Better Business Bureau. Web. 22 Mar. 2016.

Bögels, Sara, Kobin H. Kendrick, and Stephen C. Levinson. "Never Say No ... How The Brain Interprets The Pregnant

Pause In Conversation." *Plos ONE* 10.12 (2015): 1-15. *Academic Search Complete*. Web. 18 Mar. 2016.

Bridge, DJ, and KA Paller. "Neural Correlates Of Reactivation And Retrieval-Induced Distortion." *Journal Of Neuroscience* 32.35: 12144-12151. *Science Citation Index*. Web. 22 Mar. 2016.

Briñol, Pablo, and Richard E. Petty. "Overt Head Movements and Persuasion: A Self-Validation Analysis." *Journal of Personality and Social Psychology* 84.6 (2003): 1123-139. *PsycINFO [EBSCO]*. Web. 17 Mar. 2016.

Building Self-Esteem In Children. [Electronic Resource].: [Rockville, MD : U.S. Dept. of Health and Human Services, Substance Abuse and Mental Health Services Administration, Center for Mental Health Services], 2003. Milner Library Only. Web. 18 Mar. 2016.

Button, Eric J., Philippa Loan, Jo Davies, and Edmund J. S. Sonuga-Barke. "Self-Esteem, Eating Problems, and Psychological Well-Being in a Cohort of Schoolgirls Aged 15-16: A Questionnaire and Interview Study." International Journal of Eating Disorders 21.1 (1997): 39-47. Web. 23 Mar. 2016.

Carroll, Patrick J. "Upward Self-Revision: Constructing Possible Selves." *Basic and Applied Social Psychology* 36.5 (2014): 377-85. *PsycINFO [EBSCO]*. Web. 17 Mar. 2016.

Clayton, Russell. "Want a Better Work-life Balance? Exercise, Study Finds." *ScienceDaily*. ScienceDaily, 9 Jan. 2014. Web. 17 Mar. 2016.

Cohen, Geoffrey L., and David K. Sherman. "The Psychology of Change: Self-Affirmation and Social Psychological Intervention." *Annual Review of Psychology*. 65.1 (2014): 333-71. *PsycINFO [EBSCO]*. Web. 17 Mar. 2016.

Costa-Giomi, Eugenia. "Effects of Three Years of Piano Instruction on Children's Academic Achievement, School Performance and Self-Esteem." *Psychology of Music* 32.2 (2004): 139-52. *PsycINFO [EBSCO]*. Web. 17 Mar. 2016.

Damisch, Lysann, Barbara Stoberock, and Thomas Mussweiler. "Keep Your Fingers Crossed!: How Superstition Improves Performance." *Psychological Science* 21.7 (2010): 1014-020. *PsycINFO [EBSCO]*. Web. 17 Mar. 2016.

Donnellan, M. Brent, Kali H. Trzesniewski, Richard W. Robins, Terrie E. Moffitt, and Avshalom Caspi. "Low Self-Esteem Is Related to Aggression, Antisocial Behavior, and Delinquency." Psychological Science 16.4 (2005): 328-35. Web. 24 Mar. 2016.

Dr. Sorenson. "Symptoms of Low Self-Esteem." *Symptoms of Low Self-Esteem*. The Self Esteem InstituteTM. Web. 19 Mar. 2016.

Epley, Nicholas, and Juliana Schroeder. "Mistakenly Seeking Solitude." *Journal of Experimental Psychology: General* 143.5 (2014): 1980-999. *PsycINFO [EBSCO]*. Web. 18 Mar. 2016.

Feeney, Nolan. "7 of Roger Ebert's Most Brutal Movie Reviews." *Entertainment - Movies*. Time Inc., 4 July 2014. Web. 23 Mar. 2016.

Herz, Rachel S. "Perfume." *Neurobiology of Sensation and Reward*. By Jay A. Gottfried. Boca Raton, FL: CRC, 2011. 371-90. Print.

Hicks, Tim. "Seven Steps for Effective Problem Solving in the Workplace." *Mediate*. Resourceful Internet Solutions, 1995. Web. 22 Mar. 2016.

Hsu, Dennis Y., Li Huang, Loran F. Nordgren, Derek D. Rucker, and Adam D. Galinsky. "The Music of Power: Perceptual and Behavioral Consequences of Powerful Music." *Social Psychological and Personality Science* 6 (2015): 75-83. *PsycINFO [EBSCO]*. Web. 17 Mar. 2016.

Huysse-Gaytandjieva, Anna, et al. "Low Self-Esteem Predicts Future Unemployment." Journal Of Applied Economics 18.2 (2015): 325-346. *Business Source Complete*. Web. 18 Mar. 2016.

LaDouceur, Pat. "How to Say No to People You Care About." MentalHelp.net. *MentalHelp.net*, 7 May 2014. Web. 25 Mar. 2016.

Martin, Melissa C. "10 Tips For Dealing With Workplace Harassment." Careerealism. *Careerealism*, 2 May 2013. Web. 22 Mar. 2016.

Masters, Brian. *Positive Thinking: Easy Self Help Guide: How to Stop Negative Thoughts, Negative Self-talk, and Reduce Stress Using the Power of Positive Thinking, Happiness, Affirmations, and Positive Psychology*. Amazon, 2016. Print.

Murphy, Nikelle. "The 5 Best Ways to Say 'No' to Your Co-workers." *Career Advice*. The Cheat Sheet, 18 Jan. 2016. Web. 22 Mar. 2016.

Nair, Shwetha, Mark Sagar, John Sollers, Nathan Consedine, and Elizabeth Broadbent. "Do Slumped and Upright Postures

Affect Stress Responses? A Randomized Trial." *Health Psychology* 34.6 (2015): 632-41. *PsycINFO [EBSCO]*. Web. 17 Mar. 2016.

Northwestern MutualVoice Team. "7 Tips For Lending Money To Family." *Forbes - Investing*. Forbes, 22 July 2014. Web. 21 Mar. 2016.

Orth, Ulrich, Richard W. Robins, Kali H. Trzesniewski, Jürgen Maes, and Manfred Schmitt. "Low Self-Esteem Is a Risk Factor for Depressive Symptoms from Young Adulthood to Old Age." Journal of Abnormal Psychology 118.3 (2009): 472-78. Web. 24 Mar. 2016.

Schiraldi, Glenn R. *10 Simple Solutions for Building Self-Esteem: How to End Self-Doubt, Gain Confidence, and Create a Positive Self-Image*. Oakland, CA: New Harbinger Publications, 2007. Print.

Shute, Nancy. "Our Brains Rewrite Our Memories, Putting Present In The Past." *Your Health*. NPR, 6 Feb. 2014. Web. 22 Mar. 2016.

Slide, Casey. "10 Reasons Why You Should NOT Lend Money to Friends & Family." *Money Crashers*. SparkCharge Media. Web. 21 Mar. 2016.

Social Anxiety Support. "*Social Anxiety Disorder and Social Phobia*." Social Anxiety Disorder and Social Phobia. Social Anxiety Support, 2008. Web. 23 Mar. 2016.

Stalter, Harmony. *Employee Body Language Revealed: How to Predict Behavior in the Workplace by Reading and Understanding Body Language.* Ocala, FL: Atlantic Pub. Group, 2011. Print.

Tartakovsky, Margarita. "Why Saying No in Your Relationship Is a Good Thing." *World of Psychology.* PsychCentral, 2012. Web. 25 Mar. 2016.

Trzesniewski, Kali H., M. Brent Donnellan, Terrie E. Moffitt, Richard W. Robins, Richie Poulton, and Avshalom Caspi. "Low Self-Esteem During Adolescence Predicts Poor Health, Criminal Behavior, and Limited Economic Prospects During Adulthood." Developmental Psychology 42.2 (2006): 381-90. Web. 22 Mar. 2016.

Vigil, Jacob Miguel. "A Socio-Relational Framework of Sex Differences in the Expression of Emotion." *Behavioral and Brain Sciences* 32.05 (2009): 375-90. *PsycINFO [EBSCO].* Web. 18 Mar. 2016.

Index